IMAGES OF WAR
U-BOAT PREY: MERCHANT SAILORS AT WAR 1939-1942

RARE PHOTOGRAPHS FROM WARTIME ARCHIVES

PHILIP KAPLAN

WITH JACK CURRIE

Pen & Sword
MARITIME

First printed in Great Britain in 2014 by
Pen & Sword Maritime
an imprint of
Pen & Sword Books Ltd.
47 Church Street
Barnsley,
South Yorkshire
S70 2AS

A CIP record for this book is available from the British Library.

ISBN 978 1 78 346 2940

The right of Philip Kaplan to be identified as Author of this Work has been asserted by him in accordance with the Copyright, Designs and Patents Act 1988.

All rights reserved. No part of this book may be reproduced or transmitted in any form or by any means, electronic or mechanical including photocopying, recording or by any information storage and retrieval system, without permission from the Publisher in writing.

Printed and bound in England
By CPI Group (UK) Ltd. Croydon, CR0 4YY

Pen & Sword Books Ltd incorporates the Imprints of Pen & Sword Aviation, Pen & Sword Family History, Pen & Sword Maritime, Pen & Sword Military, Pen & Sword Discovery, Wharncliffe Local History, Wharncliffe True Crime, Wharncliffe Transport, Pen & Sword Select, Pen & Sword Military Classics, Leo Cooper, The Praetorian Press, Remember When, Seaforth Publishing and Frontline Publishing.

For a complete list of Pen & Sword titles please contact Pen & Sword Books Limited
47 Church Street, Barnsley, South Yorkshire, S70 2AS, England

E-mail: enquiries@pen-and-sword.co.uk
Website: www.pen-and-sword.co.uk

Contents

MERCHANTMEN 3
MERCHANT SAILORS 22
HUNTERS 38
WILL SHE STARVE? 60
LIBERTY SHIPS 70
THE HUNTED 84
TANKER 101
A CADET'S STORY 114

Reasonable efforts have been made to trace the copyright holders of all material used in this book. The author apologizes for any omissioins. All reasonable efforts will be made in future editions to correct any such omissions. The author is grateful to the following people for the use of their published and/or unpublished material, or for their kind assistance in the preparation of this book: Christine Ammer, Jack Armstrong, Brooks Atkinson, Robert Atkinson, Francis Bacon, Malcolm Bates, Charles Bishop, William Bourner, Samuel Butler, George Gordon Lord Byron, Winston S. Churchill, Samuel T. Coleridge, Joseph Conrad, Jack Currie (for his text), Peter Donnelly, Dwight D, Eisenhower, Joseph Fabry, The Falkirk Herald, James E. Flecker, Sir Humphrey Gilbert, Kenneth Grahame, Charles Graves, Peter Guy, H.G. Hall, Cyril Hatton, Thom Hendrickson, Charles Hill, Samuel Johnson, Joseph J. Kaplan, Neal B. Kaplan, Ernest J. King, Rudyard Kipling, Collie Knox, Frank Knox, John Lester, Steven Levingston, Peter Lewis, Peter MacDonald, Otto Marchica, Edwin Markham, John Masefield, Wilson McArthur, Nicolas Monsarrat, Eugene O'Niell, John Palmer, A.H. Pierce, C.H. Rayner, Phil Richards, Francis Rockwell, S. Roskill, Thomas Rowe, Owen Rutter, Carl Sandburg, Leonard Sawyer, Frank Shaw, Neil Thompson, Harry S. Truman, Nancy Byrd Turner, Jack Thompson, Peter Wakker, Herbert Werner, Robert Westall, W. Whiting, J.W.S. Wilson, Woodrow Wilson, Roger P. Wise, E. Withers.

Merchantmen

The badge of the Merchant Navy

For the bread that you eat and the biscuits you nibble, the sweets that you suck and the joints that you carve, they are brought to you daily by all us Big Steamers—and if any one hinders our coming—you'll starve.
—from *Big Steamer* by Rudyard Kipling

God and our sailors we adore, when danger threatens, not before. With danger past, both are requited, God forgotten, the sailor slighted.
—*anon*, circa 1790

After every war, monuments are raised to the memory of those who died gloriously. The officers and men of the Merchant Navy, fighting this grim Battle of the Atlantic, would probably scorn such homage to their simple devotion; but it is a regrettable fact that the one memorial they would care for—the refutation of the charge explicit in the above quotation—is still, after two hundred years, unforthcoming and the slur unexpunged from the annals. For two hundred years and more, these brave men, lacking the training and organisation that adapts their brothers in the Royal Navy so readily to the rigours of war, have, never-

theless, fashioned their own magnificent tradition. Day in, day out, night in, night out, they face today unflinchingly the dangers of the deep, and those that lurk in the deep—the prowling U-boats. They know, these men, that the Battle of the Atlantic means wind and weather, cold and strain and fatigue, all in the face of enemy craft above and below, awaiting the specific moment to send them to death. They have not even the mental relief of hoping for an enemy humane enough to rescue; nor the certainty of finding safe and sound those people and those things they love when they return to homes, which may have been bombed in their absence. When the Battle of the Atlantic is won, as won it will be, it will be these men and those who have escorted them we shall have to thank. Ceaseless vigilance and the will to triumph over well nigh insuperable obstacles will have won their reward.
—Admiral Sir Percy Noble, Commander-in-Chief, Western Approaches
14th August 1941

When Admiral Horatio Nelson defeated Napoleon's Franco-Spanish fleet off Cape Trafalgar on 21st October 1805, only to die in his hour of triumph, the population of the British Islands, mourning the hero while rejoicing in the victory, numbered approximately sixteen million. They were a proud and almost self-sufficient people, needing little more than such luxuries as silks, tobacco, tea and coffee to satisfy their wants from overseas. Nearly one-hundred and thirty-four years later, when World War Two began, there were more than fifty million mouths to feed, and Britain had become increasingly reliant on a constant flow of imports, not only to maintain her position as a major manufacturing nation, but merely to survive.

Whether it was ever pedantically correct to give the title "Merchant Navy" to Britain's trading fleet can probably be questioned. There had been a time when the same ships were used for fighting and for trading, but those days had passed with the cannon and the cutlass. The fighting ships, their officers and men, remained in the service of the Crown, ever ready to wage the nation's wars, while the rest sailed the oceans of the world with one main objective—to enrich the ship-owners. And the owners were a very diverse group, with their offices in all the major ports, with a wide variety of vessels, embracing *Saucy Sue* of Yarmouth and the *Queen Elizabeth*, with motives ranging from the frankly mercenary to the idealistic, and with their employees' wages varying between the handsome and the barest subsistence levels.

So the Red Ensign flew above a multitude of ships, belonging to a multitude of individuals, each with different notions of how to run a shipping business. Nevertheless, it was due to their industry, by whatever means and for whatever motives, that by the 1930s the British Empire and the Commonwealth had developed into the greatest trading community the world had ever seen, with global port facilities and a merchant fleet of approximately 6,700 vessels—more than double the number of their nearest rival, the United States of America. It was said that, on any one day in the year, 2,500 vessels registered in Britain, were at sea or working in a port, somewhere in the world. But Britain's dependence on the imports carried by those ships was her greatest weakness in wartime, when her long-established freedom of the sea was challenged by a foreign power. That weakness had been ominously demonstrated during World War One when the U-boats of the Kaiser's navy had targeted Britain's cargo ships, and there had been times in 1917 when starvation had stared her people in the face.

With that vulnerability in mind, the government requisitioned all shipping at the start of

A merchant sailor climbing to his job at sea.

Part of an Allied convoy bringing vitally-needed goods from North America to Britain in the Second World War; at right: A merchant sailor on convoy duty.

World War Two. In service, the ships remained under the management of the line owners, who acted as agents for the Ministry of Supply, and later for the Ministry of War Transport, which, on 1st May 1941, was formed from the Ministries of Transport and of Shipping. Experts from the shipping lines, with civil servants from the Ministries, formed a central planning group which, for the duration of the war, was to decide where the ships would sail and what cargoes they would carry. The owners remained responsible for maintaining and provisioning their ships, while the newly-formed Merchant Navy Pool assumed the task of crewing.

From 1939 to 1945, the names of ships built in British shipyards for the Government, old World War One vessels purchased from the United States, or captured tonnage, took the prefix "Empire", *Empire Byron*, for example, *Empire Chaucer* and *Empire Starlight*, while those built in Canada were "Fort" or "Park" (suffix) (*Fort Brunswick*, *Avondale Park*). The Canadian-built ships were owned by the Canadian government and manned by Canadian seafarers. Some did come under the British flag and were renamed with a "Fort" prefix. American-built ships were "Ocean", as in *Ocean Vengeance*, or, if they were to be manned by British crews, "Sam" boats, as in *Sampep* and *Sambolt*, and were emergency-built Liberty ships that were bare-boat chartered to the British government and renamed. The "Sam" was popularly taken to be a reference to "Uncle Sam", but the official interpretation was that it described the profile of the ship—"Superstructure aft of midships".

At any period of time in World War Two, there might have been a dozen convoys on the wide Atlantic, each numbering anything between ten and over a hundred ships, some bound for Britain with their vital cargoes, others sailing outbound in ballast to collect the next consignment. The commercial fleets were composed of many varieties of ship—fast and slow,

Convoy conferences were held at Admiralty House in Halifax, Nova Scotia and were normally attended by the captain and the wireless operator of each ship to sail in a convoy.

large and small, old and new, coal-fired and oil-fired—and the ships were crewed by men of widely different nationalities and faiths, some of whom felt loyalties which lay more with their calling and their shipmates than with their owners or the British Crown.

The merchant ship captains, or masters, were accustomed to taking orders only from their owners, and not from officers of the Royal Navy, nor of the Reserve, no matter how much gold braid they might wear on their sleeves. In the first few months of war, few were in favour of the convoy system, and preferred to make their way alone. In this they were at one with their owners, who regarded the days spent in assembling the vital convoys and attending Commodore's conferences as so much unproductive time. The masters, for their part, did not care for the discipline required. They mistrusted (and not without reason) the rendezvous in mid-Atlantic when they were supposed to exchange escorts with a convoy coming west, and they feared the dangers of collision in the fogs that were common, at all times of the year, off the coast of Nova Scotia. It was only later, when the U-boat wolfpacks began to make their deadly presence felt, that most owners and masters accepted the fact they had to have protection, and that ships sailing alone could not be protected. Although they were as diverse in their ways and opinions as any other group of men in skilled occupations, the masters had it in common that, like their crewmen, they took pride in their calling; they also tended to believe in a destiny that shaped all human ends, and to accept whatever blows of fate, and particularly of nature, that might come along.

Until June 1940, many merchant ships were employed in the transport of the British Expeditionary Force, to the western coast of France, and in maintaining its supplies. It is remarkable that, in the nine months of the operation, only one ship was lost, and that was due to misadventure, not to action by the enemy.

Then, in May 1940, came the Blitzkrieg—the lightning strike by the Wehrmacht, spearheaded by the Luftwaffe, on Belgium, Luxembourg, the Netherlands and France. Soon, every ship that could be mustered was needed to evacuate the bulk of the BEF, along with many French soldiers, from the beaches of Dunkirk, and to bring detachments home from Calais, Brest, St Nazaire, Le Havre and Boulogne. On 17th June, the Cunarder *Lancastria*, which a week earlier had taken part in the withdrawal from Norway, was ready to sail from St Nazaire with approximately 5,300 servicemen aboard, including a large RAF contingent, when she was hit by bombs from a Dornier Do-17, and went down. There were only enough lifeboats and rafts for a fraction of the complement, and despite all rescue efforts by the destroyer HMS *Highlander*, HM trawler *Cambridgeshire*, and other ships, during the continued air attack, 2,833 of *Lancastria*'s crew and passengers were lost.

The day following the *Lancastria* disaster, the Blue Star liner *Arandora Star*, which had also been involved in the Norway operation, and had been plying to-and-fro between France and England with a weary crew ever since, sailed from Liverpool for St John's, Newfoundland, carrying 1,213 German and Italian internees, eighty-six German POWs, a military guard 200-strong, and a crew of 174. She was sailing on a zig-zag course, as was customary when a ship was not escorted, off the northwest coast of Ireland shortly before dawn on 2nd July when she was hit by a torpedo launched from Kapitänleutnant Günther Prien's *U47*. The *Arandora Star* went down with 750 of her passengers, her Captain, twelve officers and forty-two members of her crew.

The so-called "phoney war", which, for the men of the Royal and Merchant Navies, had never been anything but in deadly earnest, was over, and now its reality was clear to all the

below: Wrens working in the Operations Plotting Room at Naval Services Headquarters, Ottowa, December 1943; right: Admiral Sir Max Horton was a British submariner in World War One and Commander-in-Chief of the Western Approaches during the latter part of World War Two.

world. Materially and physically supported by her Commonwealth and Empire, and morally at least by the majority of Americans, Britain was left to carry on the fight against a rampant Germany, now joined by an opportunist Italy, and with access to captured bases stretching from Norway to the Spanish border. In July 1940, two outward-bound convoys, CW7 and CW8, were attacked in the English Channel by E-boats (German motor torpedo-boats) and bombers. In that month, forty Allied cargo ships were sunk by air attack alone. The ports of Dover, Weymouth, Portland, Plymouth and Cardiff were all heavily bombed, and inbound vessels had to be re-routed to the Bristol Channel, the Mersey and the Clyde. Nor were they immune there from the Luftwaffe's attentions.

It was decided that the headquarters of the C-in-C Western Appraches Command, from which the shipping routes to Britain around the north and south of Irelanc were controlled, should move from Plymouth to Derby House in Liverpool, where Winston Churchill, when he was First Lord of the Admiralty, had foresightedly required a bomb-proof operations centre to be built. The "Dungeon", as it was known, was staffed by hundreds of communications and crytographic experts, many of them members of the Women's Royal Naval Service, all working an eighty-four-hour week, and it was from there that Admiral Sir Percy Noble, and his successor Admiral Sir Max Horton, directed the Battle of the Atlantic.

The losses incurred by the Royal and Merchant Navies in the first year of the war included

The sinking of the *Windsor Castle* after being attacked by a German aircraft in March 1943.

a battleship, an aircraft carrier, five cruisers, three destroyers, two submarines and 438 merchantmen, all at a cost to the enemy of twenty-eight U-boats. Then, in September 1940, the major docks in the Pool of London, the East India, the Royal Victoria, the King George V and the Royal Albert, suffered forty bombing raids, in the course of which on ship, the *Minnie De Larrinaga*, was sunk and eighteen damaged, in addition to the destruction of installations and equipment, and to civilian casualties throughout the dockland area. On the 9th of the month, only one ship of five in the Victoria Docks remained afloat. Of the four ships sunk there, all were eventually raised and returned to service. These figures were severe enough, but worse were to come. From the beginning of March to the end of May 1941, 142 merchant ships, ninety-nine of which were British, were sunk by U-boats, 179 by aircraft, forty-four by surface ships and thirty-three by mines. The tonnage lost in those three months exceeded the existing rate of British ship production by three to one, and the combined British and American production by two to one. It was not until August 1942 that the combined ship production of the Allies at first balanced the losses, and then began to exceen it as month followed month.

In wartime, ships were often required to carry cargoes for which they were not built, over oceans they were never intended to sail. Willy-nilly, they travelled to and from Halifax and Liverpool, Cape Breton Island and Glasgow, Freetown and Valetta, Suez and Tobruk, Algiers and Casablanca, Reykjavik and Murmansk, Rangoon and Singapore. Often, it seemed to the seamen that their routes were selected out of sheer perversity, as though with the intention of keeping them in danger on the high seas for as long as possible. They had no way of knowing the reason for the doglegs, diversions and re-routings that were ordered by their escort commanders or the convoy commodores, for they had no access to what was known in London and in Liverpool about the wolfpacks' movements. That was top secret information, classified as Ultra, which came from Bletchley Park, where the Government's brilliant scientists had succeeded in deciphering the German Navy's supposedly unbreakable Enigma wireless codes.

The convoy commodores were all volunteers, taken from the list of retired Flag Officers of the Royal Naval Reserve. Many were over the age of sixty, and several were closer to seventy. Their American counterparts were usually Captains in the US Naval Reserve with some

Loading and replenishing U-boats in their Biscay coastal bases; left French workers and German personnel on the roof of a U-boat pen shelter in France.

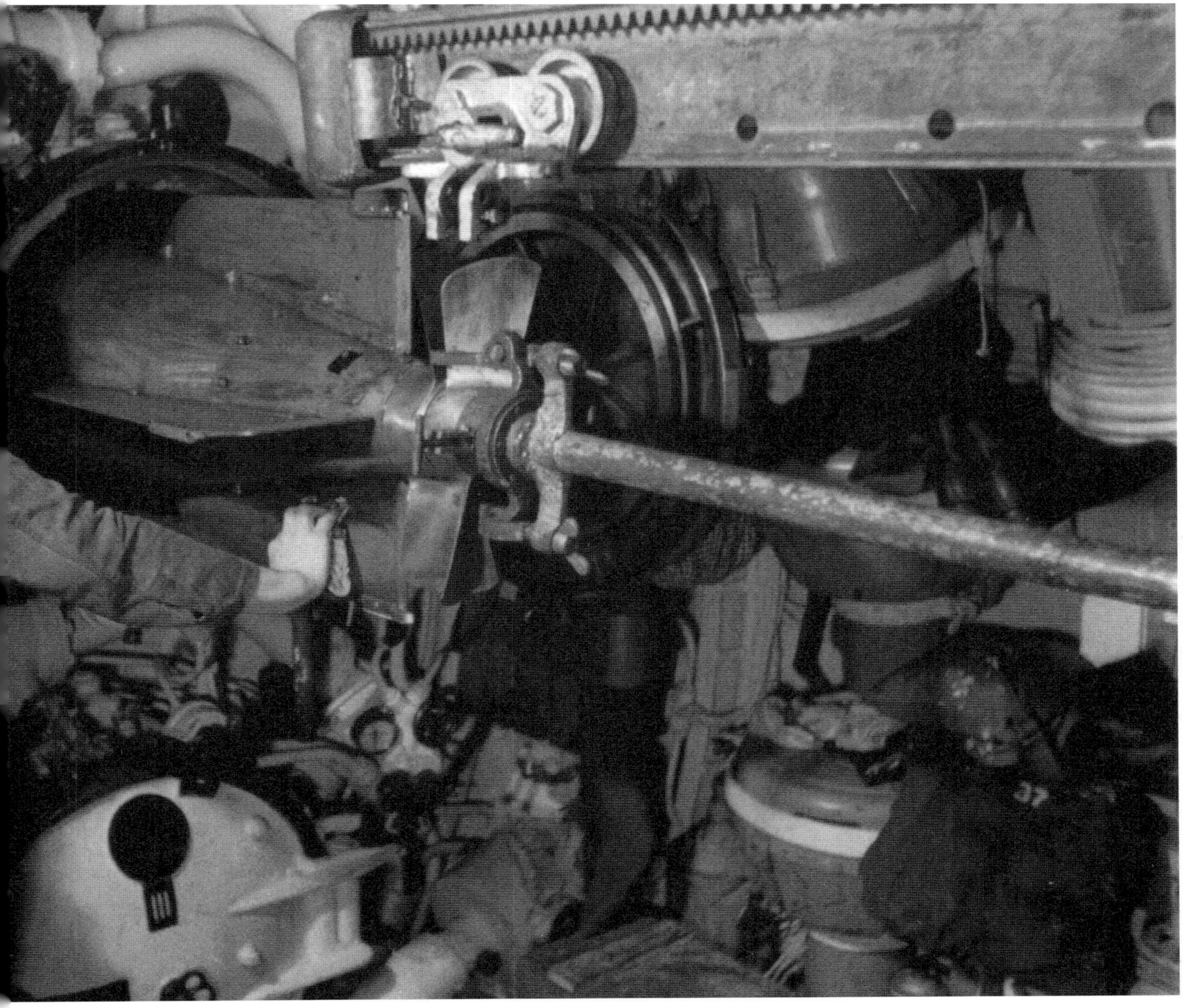

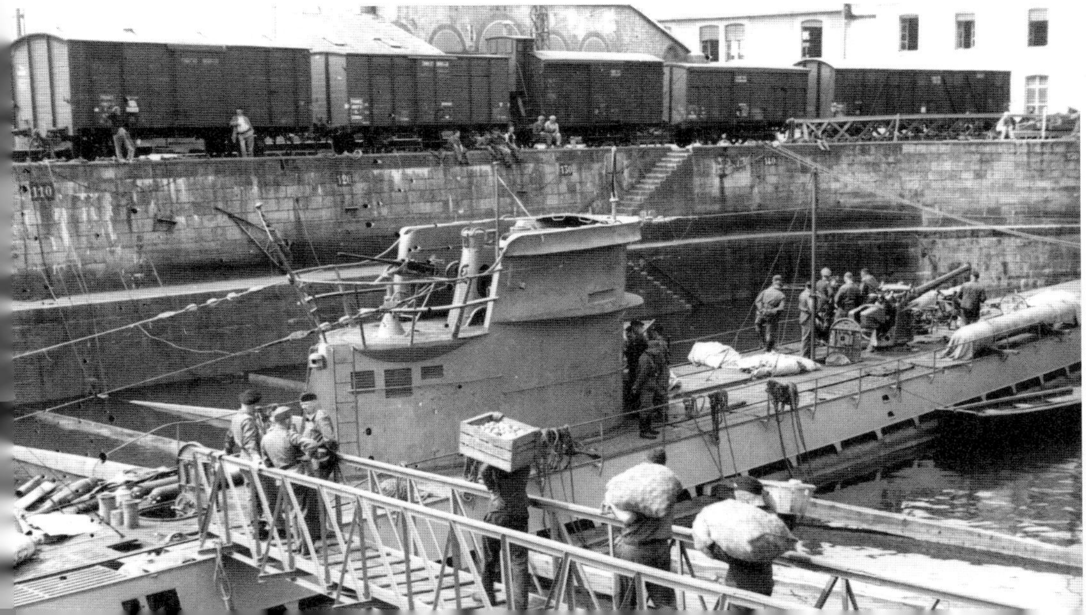

mercantile experience. At sea, the Commodore did not actually command the ship he sailed in, which was then known as "The Commodore" and identified by a white flag with a blue St George's Cross. He was responsible for alterations of the convoy's speed and course, and for close liaison with the commander of the naval escort, whose responsibility was for "the safe and timely arrival of the convoy". Normally, the Commodore had his own small signals staff, who remained with him on whichever ship he flew his flag. Twenty-one of these highly-respected, dedicated officers gave their lives in the course of World War Two.

Any merchant ship which assembled in a convoy was covered by government insurance, and some were not quite as seaworthy as they should have been. Rear Admiral Sir Kenelm Creighton took a harsh view of certain British ship-owners, who did not scruple to send men to face the perils of the North Atlantic and the onslaught of the enemy in, as he wrote, "ships that were not fit to be anywhere but in a breaker's yard". A veteran Convoy Commodore, Sir Kenelm had a right to his opinion: he had flown his flag in the cargo ship *Avoceta* when HG73 sailed for Britain from Gibraltar on 17th September 1941 with twenty-five merchantmen, an escort comprising a destroyer, two sloops, eight corvettes and HMS *Springbank*, a requisitioned merchant ship designated as an Auxiliary Catapult Fighter ship, carrying two Fairey Fulmar fighter aircraft on her launch deck. A pair of Italian submarines made the first contact west of Cape Finisterre, but the damage was done by three U-boats, which, in the following five days, sank nine of the merchantmen, including *Avoceta*. The Commodore, the master and six of the crew were rescued from a life raft by the corvette HMS *Periwinkle*. On 27th September, west of Ireland, the *Springbank*, whose fighters had previously repelled the attacks of two Focke-Wulf Condors, was sunk by *U201*.

To provide some air protection in the "Atlantic Gap", where shore-based aircraft could not reach (until the advent of very long-range aircraft), a number of oil tankers and grain carriers were fitted out with plywood flight decks, from which it was possible to operate four aircraft, while still carrying cargo below. The more conventional escort carriers carried more aircraft—usually from fifteen to twenty—with the necessary communications for their control, but at the expense of any other cargo.

At twilight on 12th September 1942, the Cunard White Star liner *Laconia*, of 19,695 gross tons, was some 200 miles off the grain coast of West Africa, sailing unescorted for England from Suez on the 12,000-mile voyage round the Cape, with 3,251 aboard, including 1,793 Italian POWs, when she was torpedoed and sunk by the Type IXC U-boat *U156*. As the U-boat moved among the lifeboats and the swimmers in the water, the commander, Werner Hartenstein, heard Italian survivors crying for help. Signalling for assistance, he somehow contrived to take nearly 200 survivors on board the *U156*, while three other submarines, German and Italian, picked up many more. It is worthy of note that Admiral Dönitz, in his memoirs, claimed the rescue of 800 British passengers and crew, and 450 Italians, whereas British sources gave the total of survivors, including those rescued by the Vichy French cruiser *Gloire* and taken to Casablanca, and the few who survived for four weeks in lifeboats, as 975. Captain Sharp, who went down with his ship, had been master of *Lancastria* when she was sunk in the English Channel in June 1940.

The rescue operation continued for three days, but it was halted during the morning of 16th September by the intervention of an American B-24 Liberator, flying from Ascension Island, followed by two more, which dropped several bombs upon the scene, one of which caused damage to *U156*. The episode prompted Dönitz to forbid his U-boat commanders

Torpedo technicians, known as 'mixers', tending their missiles in a U-boat.

in future to attempt the rescue of the crews of sunken ships. "This applies equally", his order continued, "to the picking up of men in the water and putting them aboard a lifeboat, to the righting of capsized lifeboats, and to the supply of food and water. Such activities are a contradiction of the primary object of war, namely the destruction of enemy ships and their crews." At the post-war Nuremberg Tribunal, Dönitz successfully defended himself against the charge, argued by the British Prosecutor, that this order had contravened the rules of war.

The war at sea went on, as bitterly as ever. Between 1st August 1942 and 21st May 1943, total Allied shipping losses in the Atlantic amounted to 3,760,722 gross tons, of which nearly 2,000,000 tons were British. Gradually, however, the tide was turning in the Allies' favour, and, as it transpired, May was the crucial month. It was then that the latest radar sets on Allied ships and aircraft, the new and more effective depth-charges, and above all the work of the Bletchley Park code-breakers, were brought together, first to challenge, and at last to beat Die Rudeltaktik, the tactic of a pack of wolves.

The month, however, had not started well. When Grossadmiral Karl Dönitz ordered forty-one U-boats to attack a large westbound Allied convoy, ONS5, the order was intercepted by the British and the escort was reinforced, but bad weather grounded the long-range Liberators, and thirteen merchant ships were sunk for the loss of two U-boats. Then a fog rolled across the North Atlantic, the sea became smoother, and the escort's radar came into its own. Raider after raider was steadily tracked down, depth-charged and sunk, or forced to the surface to face the escorts' guns. The wolfpack retreated, and suddenly the tables had been turned. By 17th May, twenty-three U-boats had gone down since the beginning of the month, and there was worse to come: of twenty-one U-boats sent to intercept a big eastbound convoy, SC130, only ten sighted it and only one got close enough to deliver an attack. Two were sunk by Liberators based on Iceland and three by escort ships. One of those who died was Leutnant zur See Peter Dönitz, the admiral's own son.

It had been a long and dreadful battle, and it was by no means over. There would be longer-range U-boats, faster under water, capable of recharging their batteries while submerged, but Dönitz had seen the writing on the wall, and he stated the position succinctly: "We have lost the Battle of the Atlantic."

The naval contribution to the Normandy invasion, code-named Operation Neptune, had been in the planning since 1942 and, as D-Day approached, the Merchant Navy was more and more involved. Between January and June 1944, a million US Army personnel were carried across the Atlantic, mostly in British troop ships, which included the great Cunarders *Queen Mary* and *Queen Elizabeth*, sailing independently and each carrying some 12,000 troops or more on every voyage.

Thirteen American turbine-powered cargo ships were re-fitted in Los Angeles as "Landing Ships Infantry Large", and ferried to Britain by Merchant Navy crews. Forty-six vessels, also built in California as "Landing Ships Infantry", were armed with Oerlikons, a Bofors and a 4.7 inch gun fore and aft.

Carrying 1,500 soldiers on their decks, accompanied by echelons of Royal Navy "Landing Craft Assault" on either beam, the LSIs were to form the spearhead of the invasion force. Another fleet of merchantmen, including thirty-two American and twenty-eight British ships, would be filled with concrete and sunk to act as breakwaters and anti-aircraft gun platforms off the invasion beaches, while others, with prefabricated pierheads and concrete caissons towed by tugs across the English Channel, would form the basic structure of the "Mulberry"

Top left: Grossadmiral Karl Dönitz headed the German Unterseebootwaffe; above: provisions and ammunition on board a U-boat being readied for an Atlantic patrol; left: A gathering of guests and the crew of a German U-boat in World War Two.

harbours.

The high-level meetings were over, the great decisions made, the sealed orders opened, the armada assembled—4,126 assault and landing craft, 736 auxiliary vessels, 864 merchant ships—and a million fighting men were standing by. D-Day was to be 5th June. Then, inevitably, the weather took a hand; low cloud and squalls of rain swept across the Channel, and Overlord was postponed. For twenty-four hours in the Solent, at Spithead, Portland, Torbay and other English ports, the invasion forces waited.

Some of the vessels in the mighty fleet which set course for Normandy on 6th June had helped to take the soldiers off the beaches of Dunkirk four long years before, and for them it was a triumphal return. Since those days of withdrawal and defeat, ships flying the Red Duster had been engaged in three great Allied amphibious operations—against North Africa, Sicily and Salerno—and Overlord was the greatest of them all, perhaps the greatest in military history. Miraculously, their losses of barely one per cent were fewer than in any of those earlier invasions.

Coasters, whose customary employment lay in carrying coal or potatoes between Liverpool and Ireland, had their masts and derricks straightened, to enable them to load and carry thousands of field guns, white-starred armoured vehicles and trucks for the troops in Normandy. The Allied Air Forces commanded the skies above the assault route, the beaches, and deep into France. The Luftwaffe's impact was minimal, and the few U-boats, E-boats, and midget submarines which set out from their Bay of Biscay bases, with orders to attack the invasion fleet, were harried by aircraft all the way. Theirs was a hopeless, if not a suicidal mission.

To put the Allied armies ashore, to breach the walls of Hitler's Fortress Europe, was an historic feat of arms, and Operation Overlord did not end on D-Day. From 6th June onwards, a constant shuttle service of supply and reinforcement had to be maintained. The 12,000-ton *Llangibby Castle*, a Landing Ship (Infantry) Large, which had carried 1,590 Canadian and British soldiers to Juno Beach on D-Day, made fifty Channel crossings in the next six months, carrying over 100,000 troops. The Union Castle mail ship, built in 1929, was a real Red Ensign veteran: she had been requisitioned by the Ministry of Transport in 1940 and employed as a transport between the UK and Africa, and later Canada, for her first two years in service. In January 1942, with over 1,400 troops aboard, she had been torpedoed in the North Atlantic, and both her stern and her rudder blown away; she had been steered by her diesel engines for 3,400 miles, at a steady nine knots, first to the Azores and eventually Gibraltar, where, after some repairs aft, but still without a rudder, she had joined a slow convoy for the Clyde. The seamanship of her Captain, R.F. Bayer, on that voyage had brought him the award of the CBE. Ten months later, converted to the role of "assault transport", and carrying eighteen LCAs on her decks, the "Gibby" had sailed with her first fast convoy to North Africa on Operation Torch. After the troops had been put ashore, as the cook/steward Jack Armstrong remembers: "We were used for target practice by an enemy gun battery on one of the mountains for an hour or so. The shells landed all around us, but they only scored a hit on the after end of the boat deck; sadly, that hit killed our electrician. Our guns fired back, but they didn't have the range. We laid a smoke-screen and got away in that."

A few days after Overlord, one merchant master, whose coaster had just completed her fourth Channel crossing with a load of petrol cans, replied when he was asked how the war was going for him: "I won't be sorry to get back to coal."

In his Christmas broadcast of 1944 to the British people, King George VI, bravely overcoming his tendency to stammer, spoke these words: "Never was I more proud of the title 'Master of the Merchant Navy and Fishing Fleets' than at the time of the Normandy landings, when thousands of merchant seamen, in hundreds of ships, took across the Channel on that great adventure, our armies and their equipment."

The merchant seaman's part in the European war should have ended with VE Day. It would have done so but for the action of Kapitänleutnant Emil Klusmeier, commanding a new Type XXIII U-boat, who, late in the evening of 7th May, found one last convoy sailing out of Edinburgh into the Pentland Firth, with all aboard rejoicing.

Klusmeier fired his torpedoes into the Canadian steamer *Avondale Park* and the veteran Norwegian tramp *Sneland I*, and twenty-three men died when they went down. Klusmeier was strictly out of order—Dönitz had ordered all U-boats to cease fire and surrender—and thus the Unterseebootwaffe ended the war the way it had begun, with the destruction of a defenceless ship.

On 4th April 1945, President Roosevelt reminded the American people that, on 22nd May 1819, the SS *Savannah* had sailed on the first Atlantic crossing under steam. It was also the date, in 1943, that Grossadmiral Dönitz gave the order withdrawing active U-boats from the Atlantic. That date, Roosevelt proclaimed, would thereafter be known and celebrated as National Maritime Day in honour of the wartime courage of the mercantile marine and the skill of those who built their ships. The proclamation was reinforced by President Clinton in 1994, when he urged Americans "to observe this day with appropriate programs, ceremonies, and activities and by displaying the flag of the United States at their homes and other suitable places." The President went on to request "that all ships sailing under the American flag dress ship on that day."

The British commemorated the Battle of the Atlantic on 22nd May 1993 in Liverpool and there are annual parades at the Merchant Navy Memorial at Tower Hill, London, in September and November. A 'Convoy of Trees' is being planted in Britain's National Memorial Arboretum, with a tree for each merchant ship lost.

Merchant Sailor

Steward Jack Armstrong served aboard the Shell tanker *Corbis* in 1941, and later on the *Moreton Bay*. At right is one of his Merchant Navy Account of Wages statements.

As long as I can remember, I wanted to go to sea. And dreamed, when I saw large merchant ships pass my home town in Holland, that some day I would be on the bridge of one of them. But my father, who fished for a living his whole life, was not in favour of this. My grandfather and my uncles all had lost their lives while fishing in the North Sea. My grandfather was steamed over by an English ship in heavy fog while fishing in November 1929. Then, when I was seven, I got an eye infection, which put me in a Rotterdam hospital for several weeks. When a doctor there asked me what I wanted to become, and I told him I wanted to be a ships' officer, he told me that I would have to find another profession.
—Peter Wakker, former engineer, SS *Triton*

In September 1938, the British Government, foreseeing a need to reinforce the Merchant Navy, put out a call for volunteers with experience of the sea. The response was good and, within a year, a substantial pool of some 13,000 had been formed, including navigation officers, engineers, deck hands, cooks and stewards, ranging in age from teenage deck boys and apprentices to pensioners. They were soon needed, for when war was declared, 12,000 officers and men of the existing Merchant Navy promptly applied to join the fighting service. Many of them were members of the Royal Navy Reserve, which, according to one wardroom wit, was composed of people who were seamen but not gentlemen (the Royal Navy Volunteer Reserve, on the other hand, was said to consist of gentlemen who were not sea-

ACCOUNT OF WAGES.

Issued by the Board of Trade, In pursuance of 57 & 58 Vict. ch. 60.

Name of Ship and Official Number	Description of Voyage of Employment	Refr. No. in Agreement
S.S. MORETON BAY 130169 LONDON	Foreign	123

Name of Seaman	Date and Port of Engagement	Date of Discharge	Rate of Wages
J.W. Armstrong	3/12/41 LIVERPOOL	18 APR 1942	£9.17.6

Earnings	Amount	Deductions	Amount
Wages at £9.17.6 per month, for 4 Months 15 days	44 15 4	Advance on joining	
*Increase of wages on promotion by £ ... per month for ... months ... days		Allotments	24 —
Overtime ... Hours at ...		Fines	
War Risk	22 13 4	Forfeitures	
		Cash 30	1 9 2
Duff Pay	9 1 4	Tobacco —	9 7
		Slops 1	8 6
	76 10 0	Channel Money 2	— —
		Insurance 19 Weeks	18 8
		Health & Pensions	14 3
Deductions as per Contra	59 12 2	Unemployment	
Balance due £	16 17 10	Total Deductions £	59 12 2

Dated at the Port of LIVERPOOL this ... day of 18 APR 1942 19......

Signature of Master

NOTICE TO MASTERS.—One of these Accounts must be filled up and delivered to each Member of the Crew, or if he is to be paid off at the Mercantile Marine Office, to the Superintendent of that Office, at least Twenty-four Hours before he is paid off, under a penalty not exceeding £5, and no deductions will be allowed unless duly inserted. (Secs. 132 & 133, Merchant Shipping Act, 1894.)

*When a Seaman is promoted, or disrated, wages should be calculated for the whole period of the voyage at the rate per month originally fixed, and the amount of the increase, or decrease, for the period subsequent to the promotion or disrating should then be added or subtracted. The wages for the two parts of the period should not be calculated separately and added together. (See Sec. 59, Merchant Shipping Act, 1906.)

[TURN OVER.

Merchant sailors, from left: Robert Seager, Jack Belcher, Robert Atkinson, Peter Guy, Peter Wakker, and Charles Pollard who was Chief Engineer of the tanker San Demetrio.

seamen), and the Merchant Navy version was that the Royal Navy were 'neither trying to be both.' The pool system, however, had its disadvantages: in the course of their service, the sailors might serve with a dozen different shipping lines, depending on whichever owned the ship they joined. Consequently, they lacked the feeling of belonging to a team, unlike their brothers in the Royal Navy, who had centuries of tradition, of battles fought and won, to stiffen their morale and their resolve.

When Jack Armstrong of Hull first went to sea in 1940, the Merchant Navy Pool had yet to be formed. "Seamen then weren't allocated to a ship, and would sign on with any ship they could. Signing on was for a minimum of six months and a maximum of twelve, except for service overseas, which was for three years. But the contracts were one-way only, and owners could sign you off at any time, and in any British port. Once you signed on, you got an allotment note as an advance of pay, but since no-one had a bank account, you relied on traders and pubs to cash the allotment notes, usually at a cost of ten per cent. Paid leave wasn't introduced until 1943, and until then a seaman was paid off with his wages, minus any stoppages, plus his train fare home. Most men bought their rail tickets, and got drunk with what was left. In those days articles were signed at the Shipping Federation, which was always next to the Seamen's Home, and men hung around these buildings, waiting for a ship and listening to the grapevine. It was one of the ironic consequences of war that, when the Ministry of War Transport and the Pool came in, conditions, food and rates of pay immediately improved, and berths were allocated by the Pool."

At that time, the leave allowance was normally granted at the rate of two days for every month at sea, but it was always liable to be cut short by a telegram peremptorily ordering 'Report to Pool immediately'.

On board a merchant ship, the Captain (or Master) had command; his deck officers were normally the Chief Officer (or First Mate), the Second Officer (or Mate), responsible for navigation, and the Third Officer (or Mate), responsible for signals. They shared the bridge watches: the Chief Officer took the watch from 4 to 8 a.m., the Second Officer from 12 to 4, and the Third Officer from 8 to 12. The Radio Officer was responsible for WT communications. There would also probably be an Apprentice—a deck officer under training. The Boatswain was the senior deck rating, and under him were the Able (certified) and Ordinary (non-certified) Seamen, and the deck boys. The Ship's Carpenter maintained the woodwork and plumbing above decks.

The Chief Engineer answered for the operation of the engines and ancillary equipment, the Second Engineer for their maintenance, and the Third for the electrics. These, with a Fourth Engineer, shared the engine room watches in the same way as the deck officers shared those on the bridge, and under their supervision came the Donkeyman (the senior engine room rating), the firemen, the trimmers (or stokers) and the greasers.

The Chief Steward was in charge of all catering, with a chief cook in charge of the galley, a second cook, and an assistant steward who served the officers and attended their cabins.

At a quarter to eight in the evening of 3rd September 1939, the Donaldson Atlantic liner *Athenia* was 250 miles west of Inishtrahull, Ireland, when she was torpedoed, without warning, by the German U-boat *U30*. The 13,000-ton liner, carrying 1,418 men, women and children, including 316 American citizens, was making ten knots on a zig-zag course for Canada, where she was to be refitted as an armed merchant cruiser. The *Athenia* remained afloat until the early hours of the next morning, by which time a Norwegian freighter, two British destroyers, an American steamer and a motor yacht had arrived to rescue the survivors. Eighty-three civilian passengers, including twenty-two of the Americans, were lost. The eighteen members of the crew who also died, were, like the passengers, unarmed civilians, and they were the first Merchant Navy casualties of World War Two.

We risk our lives to bring you food. It's up to you not to waste it.

On the North Atlantic with a convoy in World War Two.

Those early deaths were to be multiplied a thousandfold and more within the next five years, nearly double those sustained in World War One. By the time VE Day came in 1945, 22,490 British merchant seamen had been killed, plus 6,093 Indian Lascars and 2,023 Chinese; to these must be added 5,662 seamen from the USA, 4,795 from Norway, approximately 2,000 from Greece 1,914 from the Netherlands, 1,886 from Denmark, 1,437 from Canada, 893 from Belgium, 182 from South Africa, 109 from Australia, and seventy-two from New Zealand. The figures do not include the deaths of nearly 4,000 gunners of the Royal Navy and the Royal Artillery who lost their lives while serving on board merchant ships, nor the many thousands incurred by neutral countries.

Seamen sailing under the Red Ensign of the Merchant Navy came from every part of the British Isles, but mainly from the coastal conurbations, the Clyde, Teeside and Tynemouth, Hull and Whitby, from Bristol and South Wales. They were joined by many Lascars from India and Africa, by Chinese and Arabs, by Africans, and by more than 50,000 who came from neutral or nominally Allied countries. A memorial to their dead in two world wars stands on Tower Hill in London, close by the north bank of the Thames. Fittingly, the model for the statue on that monument was a man from Lewis, the Outer Hebridean island which gave so many of its sons to serve in Britain's navies and to die in Britain's cause.

At sea, their living conditions and accommodation were restricted and austere. In the tramp steamers, only the master and the chief engineer had their own cabins, with a toilet and a bath; the deck officers shared cabins amidships below the bridge, while the engineer officers' were above the engine room. The rest of the crew slept in two-tier iron-framed bunks below the forecastle head—not the most stable portion of the ship—usually with the firemen and greasers on the port side, and the seamen, the bosun and carpenter starboard, and they all queued up to use the head. Nor for them the comforts enjoyed by the crew of the good ship *Mantelpiece*, as described by W.S. Gilbert in *The Bab Ballads*: A feather bed had every man, / Warm slippers and hot water can, / Brown Windsor from the captain's store, A valet, too, for every four.

"It was the long Atlantic trips that were the worst for cabin conditions," said one seaman, "especially on the lower decks, where the portholes couldn't be opened. As many as eight men ate, slept, smoked and broke wind, and generally lived in those 'glory holes' with their damp clothes. The air was thick and foul, like in a submarine. It was heaven to stand up on deck and breathe in the fresh air. There was no real recreation, only an occasional game of cards—cribbage was the favourite—just four hours on watch, eight hours off, with extra work like chipping, cleaning and painting in off-duty hours. Any spare time was spent on private chores and sleep."

The navigation equipment on a tramp was usually the minimum required: a sextant, a compass, a sounding lead and a chronometer. No radio direction-finding sets, and certainly no radar, and yet, with the basic kit they had, the tramps' 2nd Officers (usually responsible for the navigation) somehow found their way across the oceans of the world.

The merchant seaman's life was one which, in spite of its hardships and its dangers, always held a suggestion of adventure and romance. It did not matter that he would never be a rich man: he would be a real man, whose wealth lay in the depth of his experience, the breadth of his environment, the good opinion of his shipmates. He was a man, often like his father and grandfather before him (for the call of the sea tends to echo down the years in certain families), who would roam the oceans, who would know the exotic fascinations of many distant places—a man who would always have a new horizon.

left: Merchant Navy gun crew maintenance at sea; below: Hard, dirty work in the engine room of a freighter.

He might suffer badly, sometimes fatally, from extremes of temperature—heat exhaustion in the engine room, hypothermia on deck—and from the sort of injuries that were liable to afflict men who habitually handled machinery on tossing, rolling surfaces. Then, he would be dependent on such knowledge of doctoring as the master had acquired in his years at sea, or could assimilate from reading the Board of Trade's "Medical Guide for Captains". But if he should be so careless or unfortunate, in his time ashore, to contract a venereal disease (euphemistically described as lady sickness), it would be considered a "self-inflicted injury", and the man would be strictly on his own.

The stalwart efforts of the Merchant Navy seamen, and of their colleagues in the fishing fleet, did not go unrecognized within their own communities—in Britain alone, at least 150 charities were dedicated to their welfare, and thousands of women devoted their spare time to converting woollen oddments into mittens, scarves and Balaclava helmets for the sailors' comfort. Such organisations as the British Sailors Society and the American British War Relief Society did rather better with a supply of woollen jumpers, socks and gloves, undergarments, oilskins, shoes and caps. In the major ports throughout the Empire and Commonwealth where merchant shipping docked, in all the Allied and in many neutral countries, clubs and canteens were opened to cater for the seamens' brief periods ashore. Nor did service in the Merchant Navy go entirely unrewarded by the British Crown. Between them, the officers and men won five George Crosses, eighteen Distinguished Service Orders, 213 Distinguished Service Crosses, 1,077 Orders of the British Empire, 1,211 MBEs, 1,717 British Empire Medals, fifty CBEs, and ten Knighthoods.

No such honours came the way of Jack Armstrong, the mess steward from Hull, but he

Cooking on a big scale for this freighter's crew.

did one time come within hailing distance of the epitome of British glory, Winston Spencer Churchill. "In August 1941, we were en route for the UK from Halifax, when there were emergency warnings that an enemy warship was approaching, and the convoy was to scatter. It takes a while to alter course at low speed, then to accelerate, and by the time this warship arrived, the convoy was a shambles. The warship turned out to be the *Prince of Wales*, with Churchill on board, sailing home from a secret meeting with President Roosevelt. Mr Churchill may have wondered why he didn't get a rousing welcome when his ship and her escorts passed through the convoy and why it was in such a shambles. In fact, our remarks were uncomplimentary, because of the panic he had caused. I suppose the *Prince of Wales* was maintaining radio silence so as not to reveal his presence, but we all thought he should have kept away from us."

For each year of the war, a Merchant Navy master spent an average of 125 days at sea. The Atlantic Battle was fought over 4,000,000 square miles of ocean.

In 1942, the British Merchant Navy had a strength of 120,000 officers and men—the equivalent of eight Army divisions. In common with his American equivalent, the British merchant sailor had the right to decline the first two ships offered to him, but must take the third if he wanted to remain in the pool (or on the union register), and, while he so remained, he was exempt from service in the armed forces. An Able Seaman's pay was £12 a month, less than half that of his American counterpart, and slightly more than half that received by a Sergeant Pilot in the RAF. The life of an American merchant seaman was insured by his government for $5,000, and his disablement for $2,000 more; any insurance carried by a British merchant

Korvettenkapitän Günther Prien, whose bold attack and sinking of the British battleship Royal Oak in October 1939 ranks among the most daring feats of the war; right: Celebrating the award of his Knight's Cross of the Iron Cross, Leutnant Otto Kretschmer.

seaman, he paid for himself. And while the British Merchant Navy refused to recognise overtime existed, let alone reward it, the American Merchant Marine paid a rate of eighty-five cents for every hour worked over forty-four a week, and added war bonus payments of 100% for service in the North Atlantic and the Mediterranean, 80% for the Pacific and the Indian Ocean, and 40% in other theatres. The British seaman had to be content with an overall War Risk Bonus of £10 per month.

A Chief Officer's monthly salary was seldom more than £30. Until equity prevailed almost halfway through the war, when a seaman's ship went down, he at once came off the payroll. Some senior officers stayed on it if they were employed by the shipping companies. The majority, however, were employed by the Pool and suffered in the same way as the crews. A seaman's living space afloat was similar to that of a soldier or an airman in a German prisoner-of-war camp. Indeed, the near three thousand who were captured found no great difference when they were incarcerated in the German Navy's camps, Milag und Marlag, near Sandbostel, apart from missing the motion of the sea.

In a typical Atlantic convoy, the vessels would move in columns, between nine and twelve in number, like an army on the march. The columns would be separated by a thousand yards, with the ships 600 yards apart, so the convoy might present a frontage of four-and-a-half miles and be one-and-a-half miles deep. "Don't straggle, gentlemen," the ship masters would be told before departure at the Convoy Commodore's conference, "and don't romp ahead. Don't make smoke—remember, one careless stoker can get us all in trouble." And, once at sea, the master of a ship which stayed out of dressing or alignment without good reason, could expect a verbal broadside, either from the Commodore or the commander of the escort.

For a wartime airman, the worst fear, short of death or maiming, was of drifting down on a parachute into a hostile country a long way from home; for a merchant sailor, it was it was the thought of being alone on the ocean, floating in a life raft, far out of sight of any land. It was this predicament in which the only survivor of the tramp *Baron Blythswood* found himself on 21st September 1940.

The Unterseebootwaffe's "happy time" was at its height when the forty-one-ship convoy HX72, in the Western Approaches bound for Britain, sailed into the sights of Kapitänleutnant Günther Prien, in command of the *U47*. Prien called in the wolfpack, which included Korvettenkapitän Otto Kretschmer's *U99*, and the slaughter began. In the next seven hours, twelve ships went down, and the *Baron Blythswood* was one of Kretschmer's kills. Loaded with iron ore, she sank within a minute. Later, in the daylight, one of Kretschmer's deck-watch called him to the bridge. "A tiny raft," Kretschmer recorded in his Kriegstagebuch or war diary, "was wallowing in the swell with an oar erected as a mast, from which a white shirt was flying in the wind. Holding onto the makeshift mast to keep his balance, was a lone man in his underwear."

It was that lone man's lucky day. Kretschmer's crew took him aboard *U99*, wrapped him in blankets, and put him to bed with a large glass of brandy for company. When he awoke, they clothed him, supplied him with food and water, and put him aboard a lifeboat from the

left: Survivors of a torpedo attack by a U-boat, a small group await rescue in their lifeboat; below: Crewmen of a Type VIC U-boat riding out an Atlantic storm on the surface.

tanker *Invershannon*, which had been Kretschmer's first victim in the convoy. With a shout of "Good luck" and a course to steer for Ireland, Otto Kretschmer sped away.

There are other stories in the Merchant Navy annals of solitary survivors, one of which described the adventures of an able seaman, whose ship was sunk in the spring of 1943 and who found himself alone in the Atlantic with a substantial piece of wreckage, one whole cabbage and a snapshot of his wife. Occasionally munching a leaf of cabbage, drinking rain water and melted hail or snow, and talking to the photo, he survived until a ship came by eighteen days later. Another story, even more remarkable, was of a Chinese steward whose ship, the *Benlomond*, sailing west from Cape Town, was torpedoed on 23rd November 1942. The steward subsisted for no less than 133 days on the small provisions which he found on his raft, augmented by whatever fish and seagulls he could catch. He was rescued by a Brazilian fisherman, and taken to hospital in Belem, just south of the equator, and lived to tell the tale. Some ten months later, that sturdy man's record was exceeded, although only by a day, by two survivors of the *Fort Longueuil*, sunk by *U532* in the Indian Ocean. Their raft drifted ashore on the island of Sumatra, where their epic journey sadly ended in being captured and imprisoned by the Japanese.

It was once slanderously said of the Merchant Navy that its ships were "manned by the pickings of the prisons and officered by the sweepings of the public schools", in which case Britain had good cause to be grateful to her prisons and her public schools. But if such an opinion was ever held in military circles, it changed in the course of World War Two. As the years went by and the Allied armies moved onto the offensive, driving back the enemy on the fringes of his early conquests, every land commander knew what his debt was to the seaman who brought in his supplies. When American commanders spoke their minds in this regard, their words were intended for their own merchant service, but they applied equally to all.

In June 1944, just before D-Day, the Supreme Allied Commander, General Dwight D. Eisenhower, said, "Every man in this Allied Command is quick to express his admiration for the loyalty, courage and fortitude of the officers and men of the Merchant Marine. We count upon their efficiency and their utter devotion to duty as we do our own; they have never failed us yet and in all the struggles yet to come we know that they will never be deterred by any danger, hardship or privations."

On 22nd May 1945, it was the turn of Lieutenant General Alexander A. Vandegrift, Commandant, US Marine Corps: "The men and ships of the Merchant Marine have participated in every landing operation by the US Marine Corps from Guadalcanal to Iwo Jima—and we know they will be at hand when American amphibious forces hit the beaches of Japan itself. On Maritime Day we of the Marine Corps salute the men of the merchant fleet."

Then, on 30th October 1945, the British Houses of Parliament carried a resolution which was put to them as follows: "That the thanks of this House be accorded to the officers and men of the Merchant Navy for the steadfastness with which they have maintained our stocks of food and materials; for their services in transporting men and munitions to all the battles over all the seas, and for the gallantry with which, though a civilian service, they met and fought the constant attacks of the enemy."

The relative calm of these Merchant Navy images in the Second World War was all too often replaced by the feverish activity, fear and excitement of the war at sea.

Hunters

What would the future hold for the men of the Unterseebootwaffe? Roughly three of every four German submariners who went to sea in the service of their nation did not return.

A U-boat crewman is drenched through the open hatch by a wave breaking on deck.

Both Grossadmiral Erich Raeder, Commander-in-Chief of the Kriegsmarine, and Admiral Karl Dönitz, Commander of the Unterseebootwaffe, would have been far better pleased if the Führer's invasion of Poland in September 1939 had been deferred for several years. Raeder wanted time for the building of a battle fleet which would match the Royal Navy in numbers, as it already did in equipment. Dönitz, on the other hand, was convinced that the way to beat the British was with submarines, not battleships. However, he had first to persuade Raeder and, through him, Adolf Hitler, and then he needed time to build up his U-boat fleet. Unfortunately for Dönitz, Hitler's policy towards Poland, as one of his senior staff later revealed, "was governed by impatience and rage". The Führer had the bit between his teeth, and there was no stopping him.

As a result, when the war began, the Royal Navy outnumbered the Kriegsmarine by seven to one in battleships (the great new *Bismarck* and *Tirpitz* had yet to be completed), six to one in cruisers and nine to one in destroyers. Dönitz's U-boat fleet totalled fifty-six (one fewer than the Royal Navy's submarine arm), and less than half of those were capable of operating beyond the Baltic and European coastal waters. However, production steadily increased and, by the first few months of 1941, U-boats were emerging from the shipyards at the rate of ten a month. Furthermore, with the acquisition of the ports on the western coast of France in the early summer of 1940, they were no longer confined to operations within range of their bases on the North Sea and the Baltic coasts, and could patrol for days far out in mid-Atlantic. Dönitz had long dreamed of a fleet of 300 long-range U-boats—a third of which, as he envisioned them, would be on station, a third en route going out or coming back, and a third being re-equipped at base. It was a dream that nearly came true in the spring of 1942, and it was as well for the Allies that it did not.

When Germany signed the London Submarine Agreement in 1935, she had undertaken to observe the terms of the Geneva Convention in regard to submarine warfare. This meant that a U-boat commander was obliged to stop a target merchant vessel before he attacked it, to order the crew to their lifeboats and, when he had sunk the vessel, by whatever means, to ensure that the lifeboats would hold all the survivors. Such scrupulous conduct, although initially followed by some of the early U-boat commanders (but certainly not all), did not last long in the escalating violence of the war at sea.

From the middle of June 1940 until October of that year, the crews of the U-boats enjoyed what was always thought of later as their "happy time". In those months they wrought havoc on the oceans of the world, and sank over 300 Allied vessels with a gross registered tonnage of 1,457,861. It seemed then that the British had no answer to Die Rudeltaktik—the modus operandi of the wolfpacks—for which Dönitz, himself a U-boat commander in 1918, had schemed and planned throughout the 1930s. Six or seven U-boats would form a "stripe" across what was judged at Dönitz's headquarters in Lorient, to be a convoy's likely course, based on air reconnaissance or radio intercepts by Beobachtundienst (B-dienst). Once a U-boat commander had sighted the convoy, he would advise the other U-boats by radio. The pack would shadow the convoy, keeping their distance, until the time came to attack—usually at night and from the darker side of the horizon.

While the British had developed the convoy system, and used it successfully for six centuries, it seems clear, with hindsight, that in 1940 the Royal Navy did not fully appreciate the deadly threat of the wolfpacks. Ship-to-ship communications were totally inadequate, and the merchant masters—a sturdily independent breed of men—occasionally turned a blind eye to their orders and made their own decisions. In the early days, air support was almost non-existent. The only escort ships available were the little Flower Class corvettes and a number of passenger liners which had been converted, by the mounting of a few guns, into AMCs (Armed Merchant Cruisers—or 'Admiralty-Made Coffins', as the seamen called them). Such a vessel was the 16,000-ton *Rawalpindi*, once of the P. & O. Line, which was sunk on 23rd November 1939 after a heroic fight with the German battlecruisers *Scharnhorst* and *Gneisenau*, between Iceland and the Faroes in the North Atlantic. The *Rawalpindi* was the first of fifteen AMCs to be sunk in the opening eighteen months of war.

Because U-boats were still thought of as essentially operating under water, too much faith was placed in the combination of the Asdic underwater sensor (later known as Sonar) and depth-charges as the main defence against them. While they were attacked by gunfire, neither Asdic nor depth-charges were of any use against a U-boat operating on the surface after dark.

It was only after the grim days and nights of the 1940s that the organisation of the convoys and of their protection began to meet the German threat. Serviceable ship-to-ship radio telephony then became available, with search radar devices, high-frequency direction-finding apparatus HF/DF (known as "Huff-Duff") for intercepting the radio traffic between U-boats, well-equipped rescue ships with medicos on board sailing with each convoy, all-illuminating Leigh lights on aircraft, and "snowflake" flares fired by rockets and suspended on parachutes to light up the night for the escorts and the trained gunners on the merchant ships. Furthermore, the Royal Canadian Navy were providing valuable aid by taking over the Atlantic escort duties as far as forty degrees west.

The construction of U-boats was a primary activity of Krupp's Germaniawerft at Kiel and, right, at Bremer-Vulkan Vegesacker Werft, Bremen, in the war years.

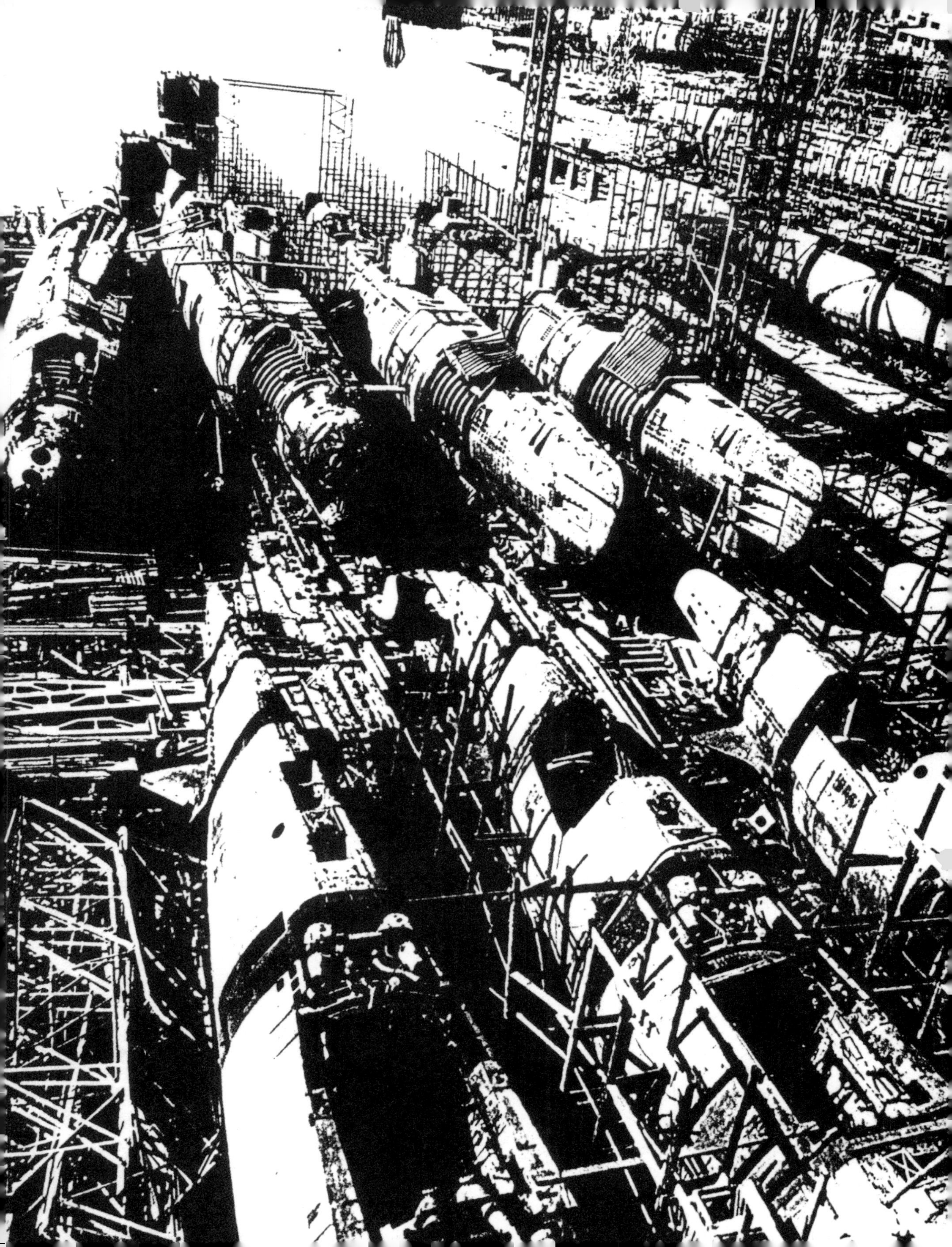

A persistent mystique has attached itself to the men of the German Ubootwaffe, the élite force which nearly succeeded in cutting Britain's transatlantic lifeline in the Second World War. That mystique is embodied in the image of the white-capped commander who took his men on patrol after dangerous patrol in their hunt for the Allied convoys, and the accumulated tonnage he would sink in achieving the goals of his mission.

45

By the end of May 1941, the German battleship *Bismarck* was one hunter which would hunt no more. Her career had been brief and not uneventful. On 24th May, she had sunk the mighty battlecruiser HMS *Hood* in the Denmark Strait with half-a-dozen salvoes of fifteen-inch shells, and, with a dozen more she had driven off the battleship HMS *Prince of Wales*. She would have broken out into the wide Atlantic had she not been spotted by an American pilot, flying an RAF Catalina. The aircraft carrier HMS *Ark Royal*'s gallant airmen in their elderly Fairey Swordfish biplanes slowed her down with their torpedoes, and on 27th May she was sunk by gunfire from the battleships HMS *King George V* and HMS *Rodney*. The event held far more significance in the war at sea than the sinking of one battleship, for its effect was to disillusion Hitler with Raeder's surface fleet, and to make him look with favour on Dönitz's U-boats.

In December 1941, at Pier Head in Liverpool, the survivors of the *Bismarck* (only about a twentieth of her complement of over 2,000) were taken aboard the merchantman *Moreton Bay* of the Aberdeen and Commonwealth Line. Her holds, fitted with iron bars, were to serve as cells when she took the German sailors to Canada as prisoners of war. "We had always hoped," said steward Jack Armstrong, "that we wouldn't meet the *Bismarck*, and yet when the seamen arrived, there was a comradeship between us. They made models out of anything to hand and exhanged them for whatever we could give. They even gave a Christmas concert for the crew. We knew they were the enemy, but to us they were seamen, and the sea has its own fraternity. Their military guards could not quite understand this."

It was as well for the Allies that the Unterseebootwaffe had on-going trouble with the guidance systems of its torpedoes. For the first two years of the war, until Dönitz at last got some action from the Kriegsmarine's torpedo development establishment, many of the German torpedoes were not detonating or were running at the wrong depth for a strike. It was not until mid-September 1943 that the U-boats were equipped with the acoustic Zaunkönig torpedo, designated "Gnat" (for German Naval Acoustic Torpedo) by the Allies, which, once launched, could home in on the sound of any motor. The British, however, produced a simple but effective countermeasure—a dinghy towed astern containing a noisy donkey engine, called a "Foxer", which fooled the Gnat's homer.

It was not until strong air support became available, and the American Hudsons, long-range Liberators and Catalinas joined the British Sunderlands and Ansons on ocean patrol, that the hunting U-boats were obliged to "go down into the cellar" more and more often, and to stay below the surface longer. Then, at last, the Asdic and depth-charges of the escort warships came into their own. By the end of the war, depth-charges dropped or thrown from ships had sunk 158 U-boats and, together with those launched from aircraft, had accounted for 42.8% of all U-boat sinkings. On many occasions, a U-boat was depth-charged for hour after hour, while the commander turned and twisted, trying to evade the next deadly salvo. *U-575*, for example, was hunted for eighteen hours, and eventually escaped, but on 29th February 1944, the long-serving *U-358* was sunk after a search that lasted for more than a day and a half.

Korvettenkapitän Werner Henke's *U515* reportedly reached 250 metres (about 820 feet), and Herbert Werner claimed 280 metres in command of *U230*. The water pressure at 600 feet—the authorised safe diving depth—is about 200 tons on each square yard.

Excellent weapon platform though it was, a U-boat under water had a number of weak points: first, its speed was cut by half; second, it was blind, and dependent on the hydrophones for warning of approach by other vessels; third, when the boat went deep, it's structural integrity was jeopardised by exhausts, inlets, glands and vents in the pressure hull. "Every noise was strange," said one U-boat commander, "and every creak seemed to herald the end." All the while, in the cramped crew compartments, the air became fouler and the temperature hotter. Eventually, starved of amperes for the batteries and oxygen for the crew, the commander had to blow tanks and face the music on the surface. Furthermore, a U-boat

The other battle of the U-boat mariners, like the merchant seamen, was with the sea and the punishing weather conditions.

could not hover: it had to have motive power, diesel or electrical, for its hydroplanes and rudders to be effective.

Because more of them were built than any other type, the VIIC, long, sleek and sinister in aspect, was the main weapon in Admiral Dönitz's U-boat fleet. Its heart was the control room, housing the attack and navigation periscopes, and holding rows of levers, wheels and buttons for steering and balancing, surfacing and diving. A ladder gave access through a hatch to the conning tower above. The engine rooms were aft—a pair of diesels, each developing 1,400 horsepower between them. Amidships were the galley, the radio and hydrophone shacks, the commander's compartment, and quarters for the 1st and 2nd Officers and the Chief Engineer; the bow compartment served as a workshop, as reserve torpedo stowage, and part accommodation for the forty-man crew—the deck hands, control room staff, "mixers" (the torpedo men), telegraphists and "stokers" (or engine room artificers). There were never enough bunks to house them all at once, so as each man came off watch he took over a "hot bunk" from the man who was relieving him.

Between eleven and fourteen torpedoes were carried, and life in the fore-ends became a little less cramped and uncomfortable after some of them had been fired and at least a man could almost stand upright. With the whole load of torpedoes, either gone or in their tubes, the men could even set up a table in the fore-ends.

The *Admiral Scheer* was a 10,000-ton German 'pocket battleship', with a draught of twenty-three feet, which enabled her to lie in shallow waters usually denied to warships with her

Below: Finding, sighting, and killing the vessels of Allied convoys was the work of the U-boat commander at his periscope; left: A Type VII U-boat on the blocks in a partially-flooded dry dock in the Biscay coast of northern France.

sort of armament—six eleven-inch, eight 5.9-inch, and six 4.1-inch guns, eight torpedo tubes, plus two spotter aircraft. At a cruising speed of fifteen knots, she had a range of 10,000 miles. She was designed to be a convoy raider, and her Captain, Theodore Krancke, knew that her task was to hit and run. When she emerged from the Baltic, and passed through the Denmark Strait into the Atlantic on 1st November 1940, her target was the convoy HX84

Long-ranging Allied aircraft ruined the day of many U-boat commanders in the terrifying Battle of the Atlantic. The Short Sunderland (above) and the Consolidated Catalina were among the most effective examples of U-boat killers employed in the Battle; left: A U-boat crewman uses a precious moment of free time to write a letter amid the foodstuffs filling the limited confines of the boat.

The captain, centre on the 'Wintergarden' of this Type VIIC U-boat, displays flowers given to him at their Biscay base in 1941.

which had left Halifax on 28th October and was reported by B-dienst to be in the Western Approaches, sailing east-north-east for Britain at a steady nine knots. The thirty-seven ships of the convoy, which included eleven tankers, were arrayed through nine columns, with the Commodore, the retired Rear Admiral H.B. Maltby, flying his flag in the *Cornish City* at the head of the centre column. The convoy's sole protection, once the Canadian destroyers had left them in mid-ocean, was the seven six-inch guns of the 14,000-ton armed merchant cruiser *Jervis Bay*, stationed between the fourth and fifth columns.

The *Jervis Bay*, built by Vickers Armstrong at Barrow in Furness and launched in January 1922, was a handsome vessel, 549 feet long, with a breadth of sixty-eight feet and a loaded

U-boat deck crew manning their gun in a surface attack on an Allied cargo ship in the Battle of the Atlantic, right, after their captain has successfully torpedoed the target.

draught of thirty-three feet. She had five oil-fired boilers, and her twin screws, driven by four turbines, gave her an operating speed of fifteen knots. She had been a favourite with passengers on the Aberdeen & Commonwealth Line until the outbreak of war, when she had been one of the first cargo liners to be converted to the role of AMC. Now, her bright colours had been painted out, her brass work dimmed, and her stylish public rooms transformed. Although many of her officers and ratings were from her peacetime complement, she was under Royal Navy command, flying the White Ensign.

On 5th November 1940, it so happened that a banana boat, the *Mopan*, sailing from Jamaica with 70,000 bunches of the fruit so rarely seen in wartime Britain, was a few miles ahead of convoy HX84, and came within the range of Krancke's guns in the early afternoon. Two well-aimed shells persuaded the *Mopan*'s captain to abandon ship, but what made him refuse his Radio Officer's request for permission to transmit a warning to HX84 remains in the realms of speculation. Unaware of the danger, the convoy was still making nine knots and steering 067 degrees when, shortly before five p.m., the lookout on a merchantman sighted a warship approaching from the north. Within moments the *Scheer* was identified, and the Commodore ordered the convoy to scatter at full speed.

None knew better than Captain E.S. Fogarty Fegen, commanding the *Jervis Bay*, that the *Scheer* had far superior speed and firepower. He decided that the only hope was to try to keep the enemy engaged until dusk came to aid the merchant ships' escape. To commit his ship to such an action—inviting her destruction—was a hard decision, but Fegen did not hesitate. He was seen turning to port to steer directly at the enemy. *Scheer*'s first salvo destroyed the *Jervis Bay*'s bridge, radio room and midship's gun; it also blew off one of Fegen's legs and injured the other. He knew his ship was doomed, but he ordered the ship's surgeon to bind up his stump, and somehow made his way aft to direct the fire from the stern gun.

The battle continued for an hour and fifty minutes until the *Jervis Bay* rolled over and sank, still with her colours flying. Meanwhile, with darkness falling, thirty-two of the convoy's vessels had escaped. Fegen, with thirty-three of his officers and 156 members of his crew went down with the ship. Sixty-five men were rescued by the crew of the Swedish freighter *Stureholm*, whose captain, Sven Olander, had seen a distress signal flashing from a raft and decided to turn back to the scene. The Victoria Cross was posthumously awarded to Captain Fegen.

When the *Stureholm* returned to Halifax with the *Jervis Bay* survivors, her master, all but one of her officers and fourteen of her crew refused to sail again. Next time she headed east out of Halifax, it was with her 2nd Officer in command and a crew made up from British survivors of HX84. She was torpedoed by *U96* in mid-Atlantic and there were no survivors.

For Captain Krancke, the HX84 sortie had not resulted in the devastating slaughter that was expected of him in Wilhelmshaven and Berlin. On Krancke's next patrol, beginning in December 1940, *Scheer*'s guns sank seventeen Allied ships in 160 days. It was the war's most successful sortie by a pocket battleship, and Krancke's reward was to be attached to Hitler's headquarters as Grossadmiral Raeder's representative. Meanwhile, in February 1941, the battlecruisers *Scharnhorst* and *Gneisenau* crept undetected through the Skagerrak into the North Atlantic and, in accordance with their Captains' orders, carefully avoiding any convoy escorted by a British warship, sank eleven merchantmen. In the same month, the heavy cruiser *Admiral Hipper* left her anchorage in Brest and set course for the Atlantic. 200 miles south-east of the Azores, she found the slow, unprotected nine-ship convoy SL64, homeward bound from Freetown, Sierra Leone. There were those on the merchant ships who identified the big ship approaching fast from the stern as the battlecruiser HMS *Renown*, which had been at anchor in Freetown when they left, come to give them escort, but they were quickly disillusioned when the German naval ensign was hoisted to *Hipper*'s masthead and she opened a devastating fire. By the time she moved away, and before a distress call could alert an avenging British warship, seven ships were sunk, two were badly damaged, and only one reached port.

And now the enemy hunters were becoming more numerous, and more widely spread. Six well-armed German surface raiders, *Pinguin* and *Atlantis*, *Komet* and *Orion*, *Kormoran* and *Thor*, disguised as neutral merchant ships, and serviced by supply ships lying close to neutral shores, roamed the seas and *Pinguin* was a menace in the Indian Ocean until 8th May 1941,

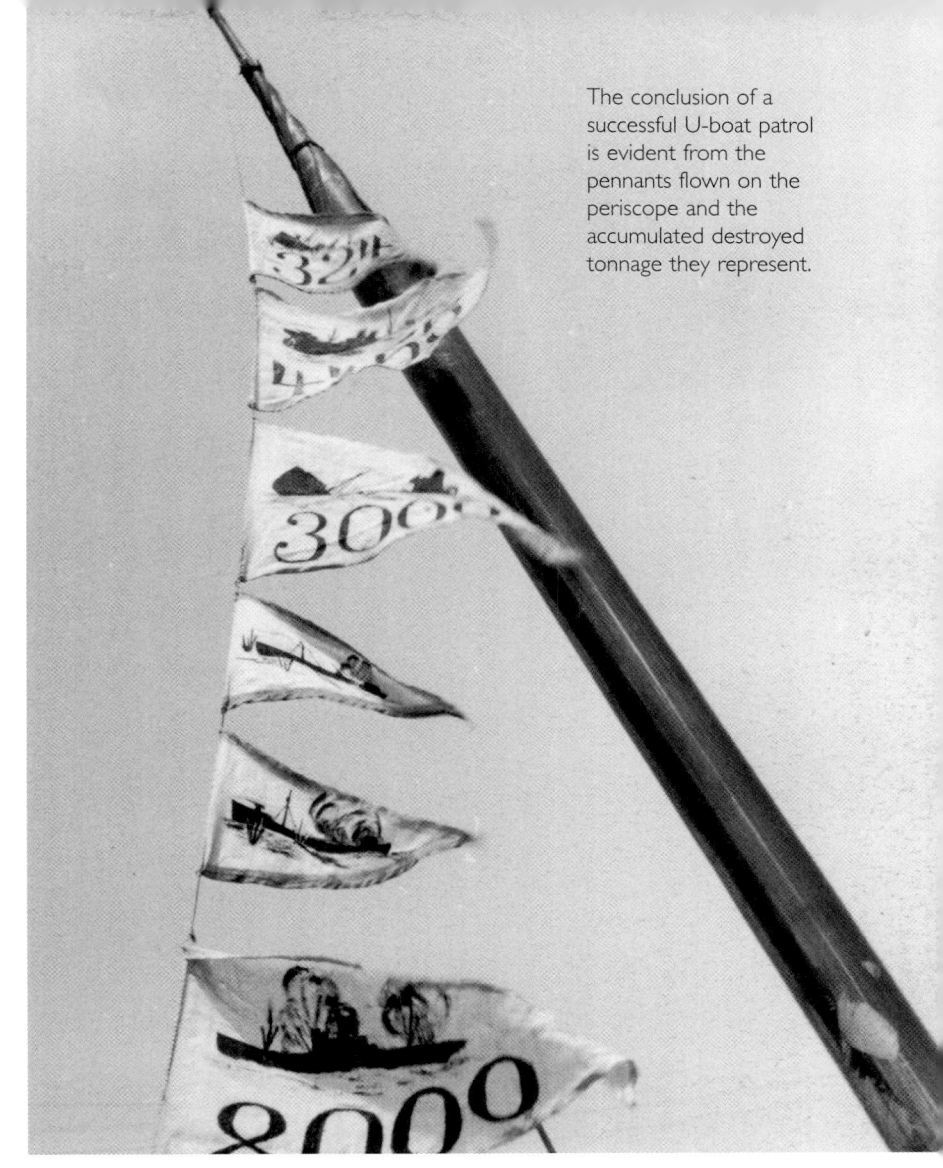

The conclusion of a successful U-boat patrol is evident from the pennants flown on the periscope and the accumulated destroyed tonnage they represent.

when the heavy cruiser HMS *Cornwall* sent her down, sadly with some 200 Merchant Navy prisoners held below her decks. When *Thor* returned to Hamburg in April, her twelve kills in the South Atlantic included HMS *Voltaire*, the last armed merchant cruiser to be lost (the AMCs were withdrawn from fighting service soon after she went down and converted into troop ships). *Komet* was guided by Soviet ice-breakers through the Kara Sea into the northeast passage, and together with the *Orion*, which returned to France from the Pacific in August after a record voyage of 127,000 miles in 570 days, she had sunk eighteen merchantmen. *Kormoran* in the South Atlantic, and *Atlantis* in the Indian Ocean, also had their successes, until both were sunk by warships in November 1941. With their destruction, the best days of the surface raiders were over.

Thor, however, made another patrol in the South Atlantic in February 1942 and, in a voyage of four months, sank a dozen ships. Her captain, Günther Grumprich, despite Dönitz's edict, was always scrupulous in picking up survivors, and it was cruel luck for those he had aboard when, at the end of his patrol, he entered a Japanese port for servicing and refit: those ill-fated seamen were condemned to three long years in prison camps.

Dönitz was the master of U-boat tactics and deployment; he was also well served with target information, largely through the radio intercepts by B-dienst and, to a lesser extent, by air reconnaissance. What he lacked was intelligence material about Allied planning and intentions.

Although Döntiz often complained about inadequate support from the Luftwaffe, Reichsmarschall Göring's air crews had many successes in the war at sea. The Focke Wulf Condors which prowled the North Atlantic and the Arctic, seeking out convoys and radioing their position to Lorient, and so to the wolfpacks, were a constant threat, and over waters nearer Germany, the torpedo bombers and the dive-bombers were notable for pressing home attacks.

In the Dr Göbbels propaganda newsreels, the U-boat crews were always pictured dauntlessly putting out to sea, or returning triumphantly, with victory pennants flying from their masts. Their commanders were always saluting and waving, bearded faces smiling, as they stepped ashore from their patrols to be greeted by the Flotilla Commander and his staff (often by their Admiral), bouquets of flowers and a brass band playing.

After the fall of France the Germans gained access to all the harbours on the Atlantic and Bay of Biscay coasts, extending the range of the U-boats into the Atlantic by 500 miles. The British would have had a countermeasure if ports on the western coast of Ireland had been available, but the Dublin government insisted on preserving its position of neutrality. This despite the fact that the Irish were heavily dependent for money on the British treasury, as well as on British shipping for supplies, and that many Irishmen were serving with the British forces.

By VE Day, 1,162 U-boats had been built in German shipyards, and 784 had been destroyed. Of 606 U-boats destroyed on the high seas US forces accounted for 132. 40,900 men had been recruited to serve in the Unterseebootwaffe, of whom 27,491 had been killed and another 5,000 made prisoners-of-war. The U-boat pens, with their twelve-foot-thick walls and roofs of reinforced concrete, were the only places where German (and Italian) submarines could be truly safe in World War Two.

right: HMCS *Penetang* was a River-class frigate serving in the Royal Canadian Navy in 1944-45, and later as a Prestonian-class frigate conversion in 1953-54.

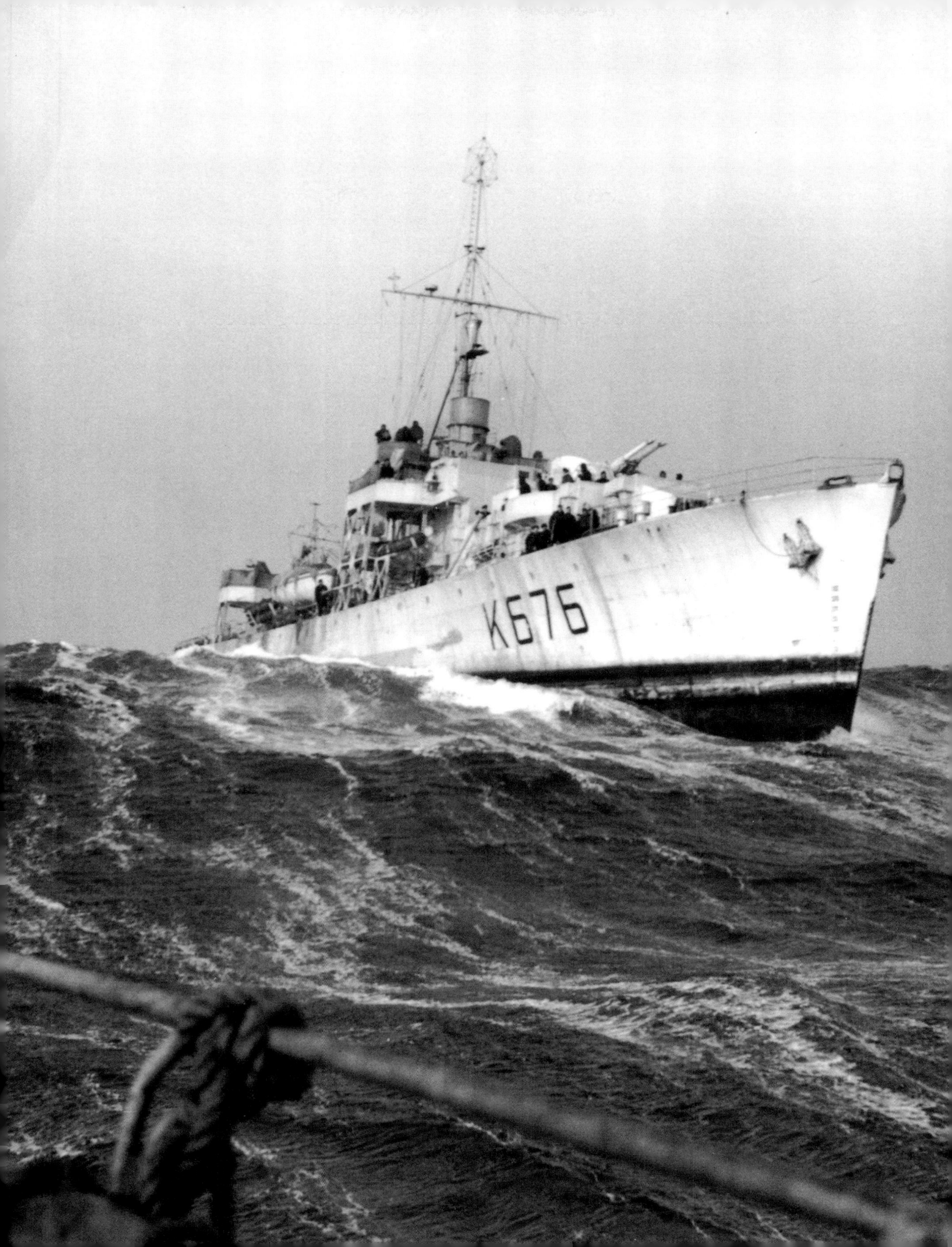
K676

Will She Starve?

German Air Force ground personnel apply representation of the convoy tonnage destroyed by the crew of this bomber; right: Many British families raised a pig during the war to augment their meagre food ration.

There were times from June 1940 onwards, and especially in the winter of 1942-43, when the German U-boat fleet came close to severing the North Atlantic lifeline, as it had so nearly done in 1917. The lessons learned then had not been lost upon the British government, and a scheme for food control was drawn up during the European crisis of 1938 and 1939. Initially, it consisted of building up a reserve of foodstuffs, planning to control supply and distribution throughout the trade, and the creation of a Ministry of Food.

In July 1939, a series of Public Information Leaflets were issued to the public from the office of the Lord Privy Seal. Leaflet No. 4 was headed "Food in Wartime", which began: You know that our country is dependent to a very large extent on supplies of food from overseas. More than twenty million tons are brought into our ports from all parts of the world in the course of a year. Our defence plans must therefore provide for the protection of our trade routes by which those supplies reach us ...

Another leaflet gave instructions about air raid warnings, the use of gas masks, lighting re-

strictions, fire precautions, and evacuation of children from parts of London and some other towns. The last section dealt with food: It is very important that at the outset of an emergency people should not buy larger quantities of foodstuffs than they would normally buy. The Government are making arrangements to ensure that there will be sufficient supplies of food, and that every person will be able to obtain regularly his or her fair share, and they will take steps to prevent any sudden rise in prices. But if some people try to buy abnormal quantities, before the full scheme of control is working, they will be taking food which should be available to others. The scheme was implemented by the Ministry of Food as soon as World War Two began, but not before there had been some panic buying, despite all exhortations. The plans embraced the issue through the Post Office of forty-five million ration books, an import programme, a trade licensing system, and price controls. At local level, the scheme was to be administered by some 1,300 Food Control Committees and Food Offices in each Urban and Rural District. There were three types of ration book: for children under six, for all over six, and for certain workers who travelled round the country.

The first items to be rationed, on 8th January 1940, were butter and sugar (four ounces per person per week of each), bacon and ham (twelve ounces); meat went on the ration two months later, with children under six allowed eleven pennyworth per week, and others one shilling and sixpence worth; meat was soon followed by fats, cheese, tea, preserves, canned foods, cereals and biscuits, and the sugar ration was halved. Supplies of extra milk, cod liver oil and orange juice were reserved for young children, and expectant or nursing mothers.

In October, at the time when autumn was turning to winter in the North Atlantic, sixty-three merchant ships went down, carrying over 352,000 tons of cargo, and every ship that sailed was under constant threat from the thousands of magnetic mines laid around the coasts of Britain, from attack by surface warships and aircraft, and, deadliest of all, from the silent menace of torpedoes launched from U-boats.

The War Cabinet's assessment of Britain's requirement for imports was 43,000,000 tons, and by October 1940, after the U-boats' "happy time", the tonnage reaching British ports had been reduced to 38,000,000. It was a serious shortfall and potentially fatal to Britain's war effort.

In 1941, the Port of London was only functioning at a quarter of its full capacity, the Channel ports were under frequent air attack, while Bristol, Liverpool, Manchester, and Clydeside were by no means immune. Winston Churchill was as gravely concerned in this arena of Britain's fight against the Nazis as in any other phase of the war. "Our losses," he reported to the War Cabinet, "are very heavy, and, vast as are our resources, the losses cannot continue indefinitely without seriously affecting our war effort and our means of subsistence." He minuted the First Lord of the Admiralty, Mr A.V. Alexander: "I see that entrances of ships with cargo in January are less than half of what they were last January."

Churchill's selection of the vital data was perceptive, as it often was: once the losses of shipping exceeded the number of replacements, as indeed they had, the future for the British people was extremely grim. Early on, it had been decided that fresh fruit was out, while meat and eggs were in. But, to save cargo space and weight, imported meat had to be boned, eggs had to be shelled, and both commodities had to be dehydrated. This meant that meat from overseas would always look, and often taste, like sawdust, and that eggs could only be eaten scrambled or as omelettes. As for vitamin C, so essential to good health, green vegetables had to take the place of fruit, and every house dweller with the smallest piece of garden was encouraged, by official posters and through all the media, to give up his lawn and flower bed for the duration and "Dig for Victory". People with no gardens grew lettuces and radishes in their window boxes, and all manner of vegetables were cultivated on parkland, railway embankments, sports fields, and bomb sites. Meanwhile, the public were bombarded with "Food Facts" in the newspapers, "Kitchen Front" broadcasts on the radio and "Food Flashes" in the cinema.

The Ministry of Food employed artists to produce posters of "Doctor Carrot" and "Potato Pete", each jovially encouraging the consumption of his wares. While offering no great threat to Walt Disney as cartoon characters, they served to get the message across, especially to children, and their recipes for "carrot cookies" and "potato pie" were generally accepted, as were others from the Ministry for such dishes as "parsnip pudding", "cod pancakes", "marrow pudding", "potato piglets", "liver savoury", "eggless sponge" of which, predictably, the principal ingredients were "1 large raw potato, grated, and 2 medium raw carrots, grated".

It was a good day for the British, and for the cause of democracy, when, on 5th November 1940, Franklin D. Roosevelt was re-elected President of the United States. He had been Assistant Secretary of the Navy from 1913 to 1930, and, like Winston Churchill, who had been First Lord of the Admiralty at a crucial stage of World War One, he had an empathy with sailors, and an understanding of the sea. It was a bond between them of which the Englishman constantly reminded the American by signing all their wartime correspondence as a "Former Naval Person".

Three days after the Japanese attack on Pearl Harbor, President Roosevelt announced: "In future, US air and naval forces will protect all shipping in their waters of whatever flag close to the US safety zone."

The passage of the "Lend-Lease" Bill through Congress, and its authorisation by Roosevelt

500
Wartime
Recipes
Food alternatives, Rationing hints, and
Economical suggestions to help you serve
nutritious, attractive wartime meals

25¢ THE AUTHENTIC
VICTORY
COOK BOOK
Tested Recipes for
DELICIOUS DISHES in WAR TIME
VITAMINS and NUTRITIONAL
VALUES FEATURED
FOR VICTORY

DIG FOR
VICTORY

Come and help with the
VICTORY HARVEST
You are needed in the fields

ABC
OF
VICTORY
GARDENS
BACKYARD FARMING
MADE EASY FOR ALL
OFFICIAL INFORMATION
AN AUTHORITATIVE
GUIDE TO HELP YOU
GROW VEGETABLES
FOOD
FOR VICTORY!

BILE BEANS
For Radiant
HEALTH
and a Lovely
FIGURE

MEAT
in the meal
for Health Defense

THE New BOOK OF RATION-
REVISED RECIPES AND MENUS
Including A HANDY Changeable
TABLE OF POINT-VALUES FOR
All FOODS...
Coupon
Cookery
by
Prudence
Penny

on 11th March 1941, was acknowledged by Churchill with this heartfelt message: "Our blessings from the whole British Empire go out to you and the American nation for this very present help in time of trouble." Earlier, in September 1940, when one of Britain's major needs had been for Atlantic escort ships, a deal had been made between Washington and London which brought the Royal Navy the loan of fifty (later extended to 250) World War One American "four-stack" destroyers in return for a ninety-nine year lease to the USA of British bases in the Bahamas and the West Indies.

Meanwhile, in the summer of 1941, Churchill found it necessary to chide Lord Woolton, the Minister of Food, for reducing the meat ration; people, he protested, would be obliged to eat more bread, which would lead in turn to more cargo space being needed for imported wheat. "Let us also," he advised, "persuade the Americans to provide us with more pork." That was a year in which merchant shipping losses, including British, Allied and neutral vessels, amounted to 1,141) over half of which were sunk by U-boats), with a gross tonnage of over four million.

The Women's Land Army, first formed in World War One, was reactivated, and thousands of "Land Girls", many in their teens, left their urban homes, their work in offices and factories, and went to work on farms throughout the country. Often, their accommodation was primitive and sometimes they were met with suspicion and hostility. They received no favours and very little training, and were expected to carry out the work of the men they were replacing, or augmenting. They worked long hours in seeding, planting and cultivating crops, tending livestock, driving ploughs and tractors (and maintaining them), and bringing in the harvest. Reinforced by German and Italian prisoners-of-war, by conscientious objectors and volunteers, they reached a strength of 200,000 and made a vital contribution to Britain's farming effort. Children, too, were encouraged, during weekends and school holidays, to join "Help a Farmer" schemes. The "British Restaurants" which had been established in the Blitz

The American meat product Spam was a staple food item in British and American households, on ships and military bases the world over in the Second World War. The rationing of many food items continued in Britain into the 1950s.

Rabbit Pie — 6ᵈ & 8ᵈ
+ Veg
Braised Liver 6ᵈ & 8ᵈ
+ Veg
Steak & Kidney Pie &
Veg 6 & 8ᵈ

Sultana Roll — 2ᵈ
Rice Pudding 2ᵈ
Lentil Soup 1ᵈ
Childrens Meals 4ᵈ

for people bombed out of their homes and for transient workers in the target cities, later became a part of urban life, serving one-course meals at a shilling each. By 1943, over 10,000 British Restaurants were providing some 600,000 meals a day. The ambiance was austere, the décor non-existent, and self-service was the rule, but the food was nourishing and cost no coupons from the ration book.

Food control in Britain, despite all its complexities and the infinite opportunities it gave for bureaucratic bungling, was well administered. There were some grumbles, as there are bound to be whenever demand exceeds supply, and there was a thriving "black market", in which money could illicitly be used to supplement the ration book, but the scheme, as it evolved, was generally accepted by the public, and it worked. Indeed, it kept on working for a long time after victory was won. Due to world food shortages and adverse weather, British rations of butter, cooking fats and bacon were lower in 1946 than during the war, bread went on the ration, followed by potatoes in 1947. Despite the U-boats, and thanks to the Merchant navies, the British had not starved: in fact, the strict regime had done their health no harm, but it was a happy day, in 1954, when the last ration book was thrown away.

Dig! Dig! Dig! And your muscles will grow big, / Keep on pushing the spade! / Don't mine the worms, / Just ignore their squirms, / And when your back aches / laugh with glee / And keep on diggin' / Till we give our foes a wiggin' / Dig! Dig! Dig! to victory.
—a song of World War Two (It applied in America as well!)

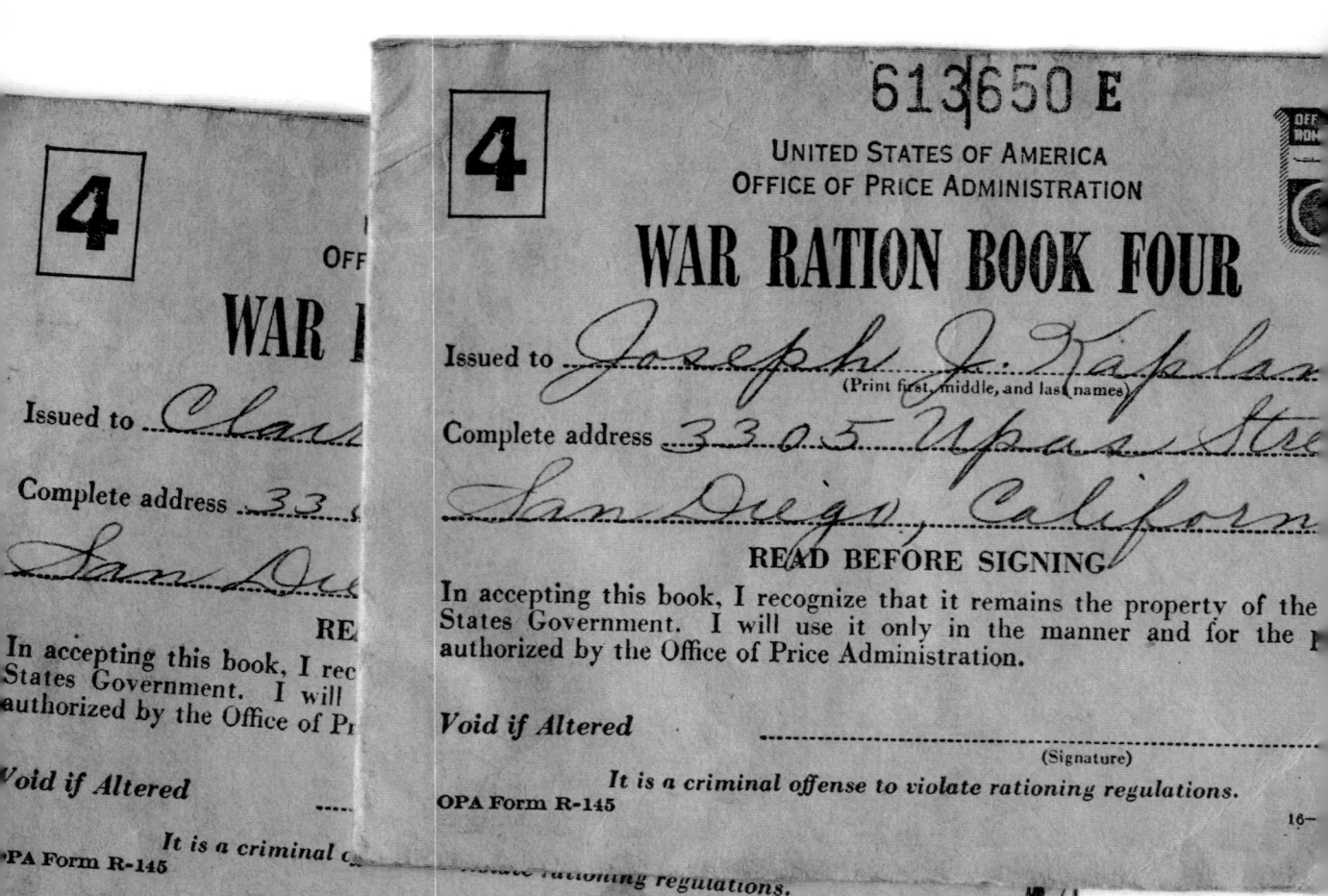

The lorry would arrive in the docks for, say 100 sides of beef and the checker would ask him if he wanted some extras. If he was that way inclined he'd take 110, sign for 100 and then, on the way to Smithfield, drop the extra lot off at a butcher's shop.
—from *A People's War* by Peter Lewis

When you could buy sweets they came wrapped in a cone of newspaper like fish and chips did. You tore the newspaper in half afterwards to use in the lavatory.
—from *When I Was Young* by Neil Thomson

Liver Savoury
Chop ? lb (100 g) liver into small pieces, coat them with flour and fry in dripping Cover four slices of stale bread with sliced tomatoes, sprinkle with grated cheese, dot with. little lumps of fat and grill quickly. Place the fried liver pieces on top of the grilled bread and serve.

123 Skirly-Mirly
Boil equal quantities of peeled potatoes and peeled swedes seperately in salted water until tender. Drain well. Mash the potatoes and swedes into a smooth paste and mix well. Add a little hot milk and margarine to taste. Season with pepper. Serve piled in a hot vegetable dish.

Liberty Ships

A British design concept, the Liberty ship was a cargo carrier constructed in the U.S. Cheap and quick to build, the Liberty was soon to symbolize the might of American industrial output.

Among America's contributions to the Allied cause, her industry's production of cargo ships, and indeed of warships, must stand high upon the list. Even before the United States came into the war, she had provided Britain with sixty Ocean-type cargo ships, and these were soon followed by fifty (ultimately 250) old and barely seaworthy, but useful "four-pipe" destroyers. Thereafter, the massive expansion of the American ship-building industry was far beyond the capacity of any other country. In 1942, new shipping built for Britain, totalled over 5,000,000 tons, rising to over 12,000,000 tons in 1943.

Eighteen new yards, with a total of 171 shipways, were dedicated by the Commission to the construction of the so-called "Liberty" EC-2 general cargo ships, each of 7,176 gross

The *Jeremiah O'Brien* is one of the last two remaining examples of the World War Two Liberty ship.

tons and 10,500 tons deadweight, with an overall length of 441 feet seven inches, five cargo holds, a beam of fifty-six feet ten inches, a draught (loaded) of twenty-seven feet seven inches, a range of 17,000 miles and a speed of eleven knots. The normal crew consisted of the master, nine officers, two or three cadets, the bosun, the purser, the carpenter, and forty-eight men. The original design was British, from the Sunderland firm of J.L. Thompson, but the Americans simplified the structure, using many prefabricated parts and replaced riveting with welding. As an example of how welding the hull plates speeded up the process, a fifty-way shipyard in 1919 built sixty-nine riveted ships totalling 517,000 deadweight tons, whereas a twelve-way Maritime Commission yard in 1943 turned out 205 welded ships of 2,150,000 tons. Each ship contained 121,000 board feet of timber, 72,000 square feet of plywood, a water distillation system, and could carry 440 light tanks or 2,840 Jeeps.

The first Liberty ship, named the *Patrick Henry*, took 244 days to build. The ship was sponsored by Mrs Henry Wallace, wife of the Vice-President, and was launched in Baltimore on 27th September 1941 and delivered on 31st December. She was to sail 90,000 miles and to carry 110,000 tons of cargo in every theatre of war except the Asiatic. On the run to Murmansk, she was targeted by aircraft and by U-boats, but escaped; later, off North Africa, she suffered bomb and bullet damage, but throughout her life at sea she never needed a major overhaul of hull or machinery.

By 1944 the average time for construction of a Liberty ship had been reduced to forty-two days, and 140 vessels were being launched every month. By then, women were forming eighteen per cent of the workforce, forty skilled trades were involved in the process, and 36,000 houses, costing $40,000,000. were put up around the shipyards to accommodate the workers.

The Liberty ships were not the most beautiful of vessels (President Roosevelt once described them as "dreadful-looking objects"), but their cost—$2,000,000. per hull—was low, and their prefabricated parts and welded plates made them particularly suitable for mass assembly. Furthermore, they came along at exactly the right time—a time when Britain's shipping losses were exceeding her capacity for replacement.

Of the industrialists who set up assembly plants throughout the USA to turn out the Liberty ships, and who vied with one another to produce the most, perhaps the best known was Henry J. Kaiser, a Californian civil engineer who knew all there was to know about building dams and bridges but, it was rumoured, could neither tell port from starboard nor stem from stern. His expertise lay in the field of mass production, and, as a result of his and other shipyard owners' efforts, by October 1945, when the last, the *Albert M. Boe* (named after a chief engineer who had died a hero's death at sea), was delivered, 2,751 Liberty ships had been built in Maritime Commission yards. These were in addition to 450 C-type cargo ships, 550 T-2 or T-3 ocean-going tankers and, beginning in February 1944, over 300 VC-2 "Victory" general cargo ships.

The Victory ships were built to a Maritime Commission design, and although they were slightly larger, they took even less time to construct. Powered by turbines instead of steam engines, they were fifty per cent faster and had a slightly longer range. After the first, the *United Victory*, whose service life was spent in the Pacific theatre, thirty-five Victory ships were named for the Allied nations and the rest for towns, cities, universities and colleges in the United States.

At the height of the construction programme, one Liberty ship, the *Robert G. Peary* (most

The Liberty ship

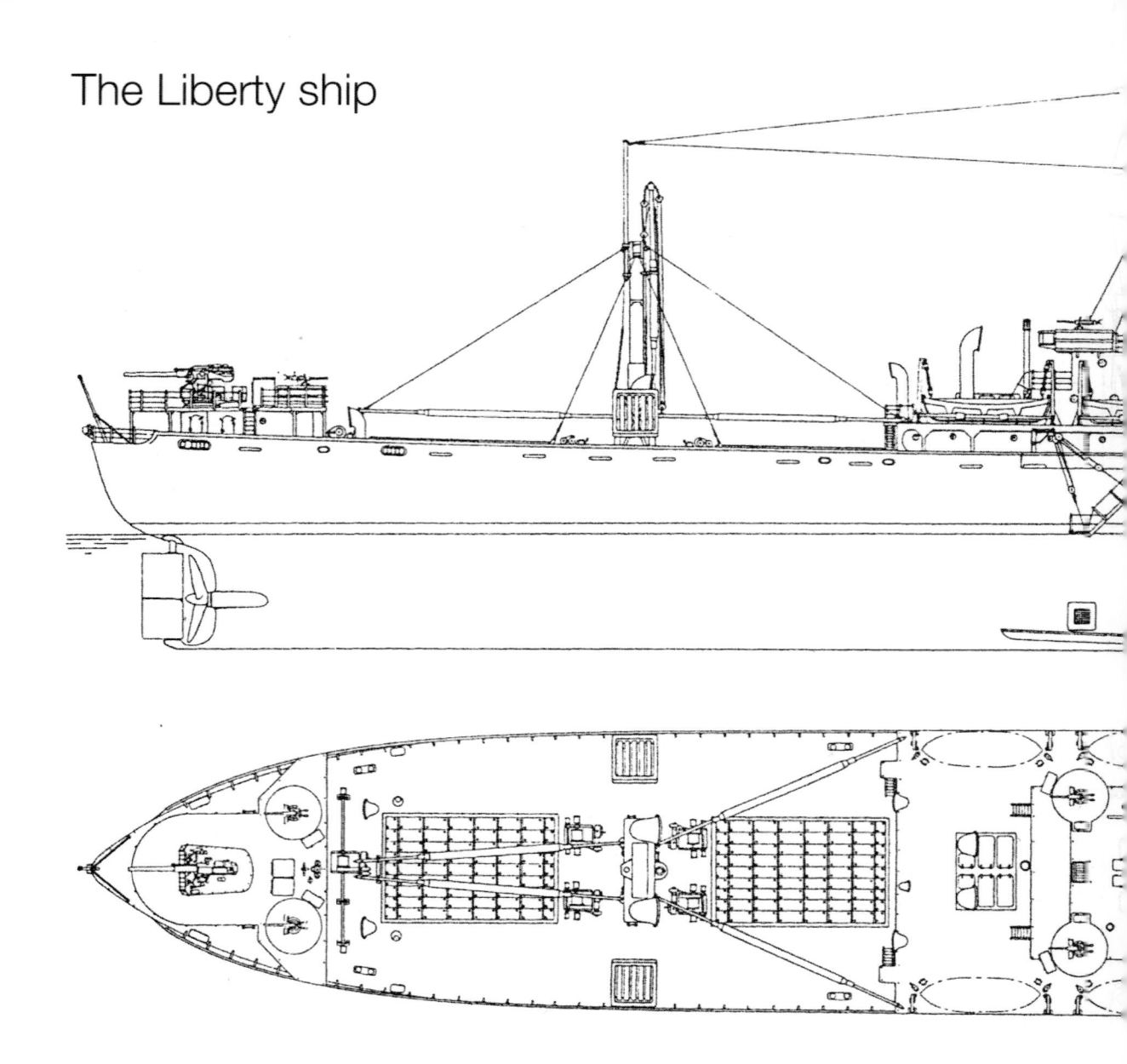

Liberty ships were named after prominent American citizens), was completed within four days and fifteen-and-a-half hours of her keel being laid, and was fitted out ready for sailing three days later. One lady who had been invited to christen one of the Liberty ships, was standing ready for the launching with a champagne bottle in her hand when she noticed that the keel had yet to be laid. She enquired of Henry Kaiser what he thought she ought to do. "Just start swinging, Ma'am," he replied.

The American *Christopher Newport* was one of seven Liberty ships in the ill-fated convoy PQ17 which set out from Iceland for Murmansk on 27th June 1942. Patrolling U-boats first made contact with the convoy on 2nd July, sixty miles west of Bear Island; but their attacks were repulsed by the strong destroyer escort. Later in the day, eight torpedo-bombers were also driven off and, on the next day, twenty-six more were frustrated by low cloud. In the early hours of 4th July, a Heinkel 115 appeared out of the fog which lay like a blanke above the mastheads of the convoy, and aimed a torpedo at the anti-aircraft ship *Palomares*, before climbing steeply back into the overcast. The anti-aircraft ship's siren sounded six piercing blasts to indicate a sudden change of course. The torpedo ran along *Palomares*' side, passed between two ships in the convoy's outer column, hit the *Christopher Newport* and exploded in her engine room, killing the 3rd Engineer and two greasers. One of her newly-trained gunners, Seaman 1st Class Hugh P. Wright, manning an 0.3 machine-gun on the flying bridge, had

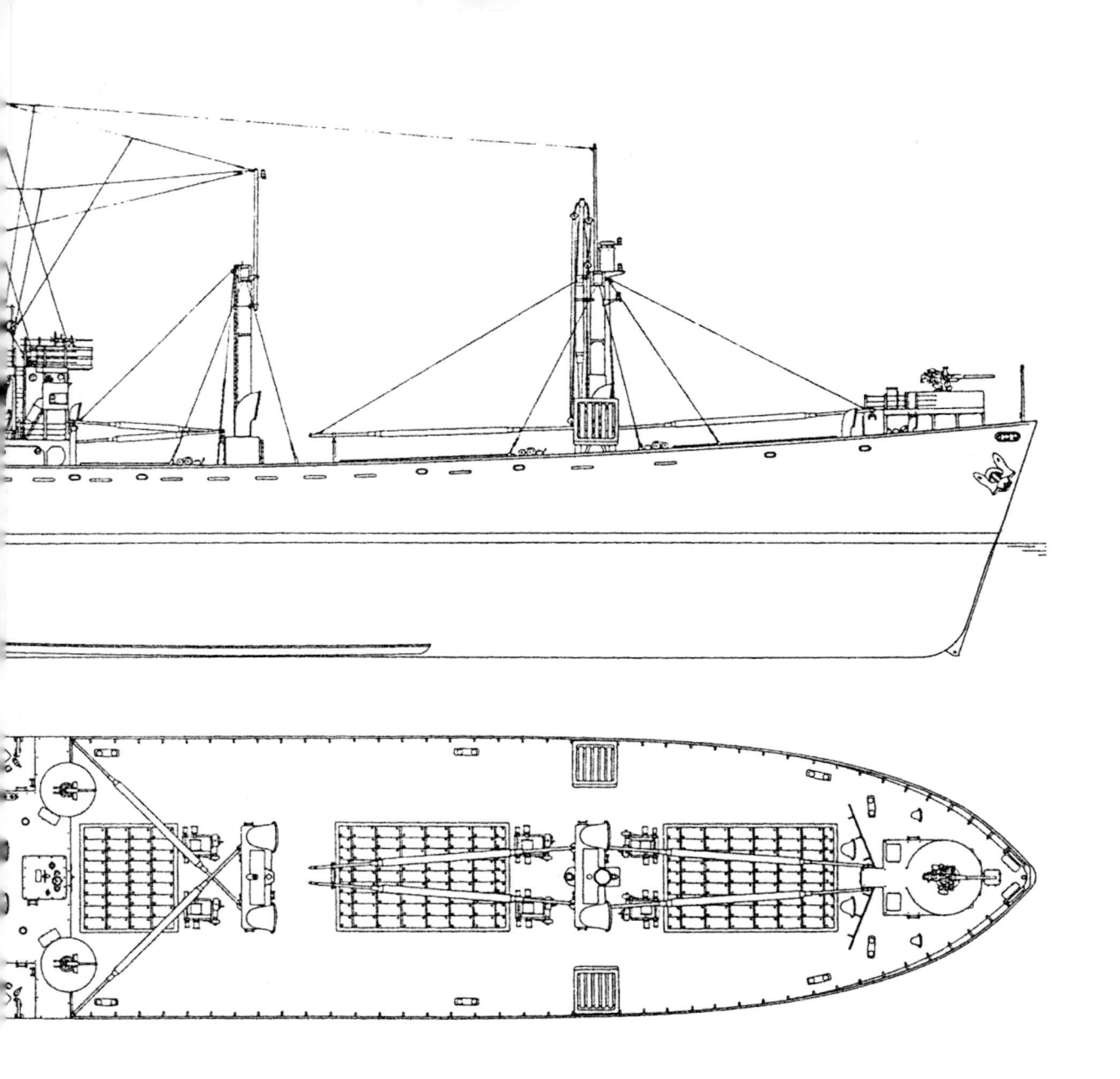

Humphrey Bogart, left, and Raymond Massey in a scene from the 1943 movie *Action in the North Atlantic*.

seen the torpedo coming and directed an accurate stream of fire at it until the explosion blew him off the bridge. The ship was abandoned, the first of twenty-two merchantmen to be lost by PQ17. Her forty-seven survivors, including Seaman Wright, were picked up by the crew of the rescue ship *Zamalek*, who were surprised to find that most of them were black, smartly dressed in shore-going clothes, remarkably cheerful and of ages which ranged from eighteen to eighty.

A well-built vessel, the *Christopher Newport* did not sink, and there were those who thought she ought to have been salvaged, but the naval commander of the close escort considered that the time taken to take her in tow would have endangered others of his charges, and he ordered one of his submarines, *P614*, to sink her. She survived, however, the "friendly" torpedoes and two depth-charges from the corvette HMS *Dianella*, and only succumbed when Korvettenkapitän Brandenburg, commanding *U457*, attracted to the scene by the sound of detonations on his hydrophone, sent her to the bottom of the Barents Sea with 10,000 tons of war supplies she was carrying to Russia.

In the annals of the Liberty ships, a story to be hallowed is of the *Henry Bacon*—one of over thirty merchantmen, mostly American-made, which were assembling off Murmansk on 17th February 1945 for the return voyage to Britain as convoy RA64. It so happened that, a few days earlier, some 500 Norwegians—the entire population of Saroya Island, a few miles west of North Cape—had come under attack by a force of Germans, and four British destroyers from Polyarno had been assigned to rescue them. The evacuation was faultlessly carried out, and the refugees were apportioned among the convoy ships. Sixty-five were put aboard the *Henry Bacon*.

For one reason or another, the convoy was slow in forming up and, during the delay, one of the escort sloops, HMS *Lark*, was put out of action by a U-boat's Gnat torpedo. Naval efforts to aid the stricken sloop depleted the convoy's defences at a crucial moment, and another Liberty ship, the *Thomas Scott*, was blown in two by a torpedo. Her crew and forty-one Norwegian passengers, were rescued by the destroyer *Onslaught*, and at last RA64 emerged into the open Barents Sea and set course northwest. Keeping well clear of the destroyer escort, six U-boats followed in pursuit.

By the evening of 18th February, a full gale was blowing, the seas were mountainous, the merchantmen were widely scattered, and to reassemble them called for a major effort by the destroyers, all running low on fuel and prevented by the weather from approaching the oilers. Early next morning, the first of many Ju-88 torpedo-bombers was seen approaching from the southwest. An article in the Norwegian magazine *Western Viking* describes the scene: "The worst storm of the entire northern campaign struck this convoy and severely damaged the *Henry Bacon*.

The *Bacon* had many Norwegians on board when she was disabled and found by German torpedo planes, but the odds caught up with them and the *Bacon* was mortally wounded. There was only room for so many in the lifeboat, and even in times of war it was women and children first. All of the Norwegians were put in the boat and saved. Many of the crew of the *Henry Bacon*, including the Captain and Chief Engineer, gave up their places in the boat so that the refugees might survive. They knew without question that they were going to perish with their ship in the Arctic Sea."

The escort carrier HMS *Nairana*'s Wildcat fighters, operating from a wildly pitching deck and frequently harassed by "friendly" anti-aircraft fire, nevertheless succeeded in destroying six Ju-88s. Other German pilots flew back to their bases with exaggerated claims of ships damaged or destroyed. In fact, all but two of those which had set out from Kola had reached safe anchorage by 1st March—the worst battered in the Faroes (with the Norwegian refugees), and the remainder in the Clyde. The *Henry Bacon* was the last Allied ship to be sunk by German aircraft in World War Two, and the conduct of her crew was in the highest and noblest traditions of the sea.

Jeremiah O'Brien was the commander of the First American Naval Flying Squadron of the War of the Revolution, and his name was given to a Liberty ship constructed for the War Shipping Administration at South Portland, Maine, and launched on 19th June 1943. She sailed on four Atlantic convoys, made eleven shuttle trips between England and the American invasion beaches during Operation Overlord, and ended her war in the Pacific. In 1946, with hundreds of other wartime vessels, she was consigned to a "reserve fleet", much of which was sold, scrapped or sunk as the years went by. The *O'Brien* survived, as was her habit, and when the National Liberty Ship Memorial, Inc. was formed in 1978 to find and preserve an original Liberty ship, she was there to meet the need.

    Now, when not away on her annual cruise, she is open to the public at Pier 32 in San Francisco. Wartime slogans hang upon the walls of her engine room and cabins; Loose lips might sink ships, and Alert! Your skill and devotion will win the war. Only two Liberty ships survive today: the *John W. Brown*, based on the east coast of the US, and the *O'Brien*. The *Jeremiah O'Brien* was the only operational survivor of the 5,000 ships which formed the Overlord armada, to sail to Normandy in 1994. Aboard was a wartime Admiral and many veterans, to take part in the ceremonies commemorating the 50th Anniversary of the D-Day landings.

The SS *Elihu Yale* left New York harbour 14th December 1943 for Norfolk, Virginia, where she left in a seventy-ship convoy, arriving in Oran, Algeria on 11th January 1944. From there, she sailed to Augusta, Sicily on 3rd February and on the 8th, she sailed to Naples, Italy. She departed Naples on the 12th, arriving at Anzio on the 13th with forty US Navy Armed Guard, forty-five Merchant Seamen and 180 Army personnel on board to discharge the cargo. From the time she arrived at the beachhead at 0840 on the 13th, to the time she was hit, there were frequent air raids and almost a contant shelling of the waters around her by long-range coastal guns. At approximately 1811 on 15th February [the crew] were notified via radio that an air alert was in progress. This was the fifteenth or sixteenth alert since 0900 the same day and it gave the position of the planes as eight miles north of Anzio—ten miles north of where the *Yale* was anchored.

    The general quarters alarm was rung, the gun crews went to their battle stations, the shore batteries opened fire and at 1812 a terrific explosion shook the ship as a bomb hit the after part of number four hatch. The bomb was identified by several members of the gun crew as a glider bomb. The bomb blew up the main deck and folded it back against the after gun platform, carrying with it the aft mast, deck locker, and number seven and number eight MM gun tubs—leaving a hole just above the waterline the width of the ship and extending from the midships deckhouse to number five hatch. At the time, the ship was about forty per cent discharged. Number four hold was empty—the other four were partially filled with gasoline,

The galley of the American Liberty ship *Jeremiah O'Brien*, and left, one of her deck guns. The *O'Brien* is permanently berthed in San Francisco.

ammunition, and some general cargo. Fire broke out immediately as the fuel oil tanks were ignited, and it spread to the LCT loaded with ammunition which was tied on the port side aft, discharging the number five hold. The fire later gutted the entire midships deckhouse. The ship's powerplant was wrecked by the explosion; consquently it was impossible to get water on deck with which to fight the fire. The number seven 20mm was firing at the time the bomb hit and afterwards; several other 20mm guns and the forward three-inch .50 fired for a minute or two at enemy aircraft until they were out of range. Due to the raging fire, the LCT exploding shells in all directions, the danger of a subsequent explosion of the cargo, and their inability to fight the fire, it was decided that the ship was to be abandoned in order to save as many lives as possible.

The Captain ordered the ship abandoned at approximately 1820. The Navy gun crew stationed amidships and forward were ordered to leave the ship as there were no enemy aircraft over the area and nothing could be done to save the ship. The gunners on the aft gun platforms, who were cut off from the rest of the ship, were ordered by the coxswain to leave the ship because of the exploding ammunition. The number one lifeboat, two large rafts forward, and numerous doughnut rafts were put over the side (the other lifeboats, etc. were destroyed) and the men went down ropes and ladders into them. In so far as possible, the ship was searched for wounded personnel and they were lowered down into the lifeboats and rafts. The ship was finally completely abandoned at about 1915, the last person going over the side onto the USS *SC-690* which pulled alongside of the starboard bow.

The men from all boats and rafts landed at the beach, or were taken aboard SCs and LCTs. A few hours later, at the request of Captain Turner, British N.O.I.C., the Captain of the SS *Elihu Yale*, T.W. Ekstrom, three Navy officers and eight members of the Merchant Crew returned to the ship and boarded it, but could do practically nothing as the fire was still burning in the midships deckhouse. They did secure all confidential publications which were not already destroyed and they were turned over to the Captain of the USS *Hopi*, a salvage tug which was fighting the fire. These men stayed aboard the *Hopi* that night and returned back on board the *Yale* the next morning. The ship was still smoldering and the midships deckhouse was completely gutted. The SS *Elihu Yale* settled on the bottom in about thirty-five feet of water and had started to split in half at the number four hatch.
—Roger P. Wise, USN

Sailing aboard a Liberty offered considerable comfort. The officers' and crews' quarters were all in one house, eliminating the need for men to pass over weather decks to reach messes. Officers were able to retreat to private rooms; crewmen slept two or three to a room. Officers and crew ate at separate sittings, the officers in the "saloon", the crew in another dining area. And one luxury for all were the showers, a great leap forward from the merchant seaman's traditional bucket-washings.
—from *Historic Ships of San Francisco* by Steven E. Levingston

On building the Liberty ships at the Henry J. Kaiser yard in Richmond, California in 1943: A procession of tin hats, overalls and lunch boxes, crowding into a new world—piles of steel plates of all shapes and sizes, shacks and booths, ladders and scaffolds, posters like the one

Typical crew bunking in the *Jeremiah O'Brien*.

reminding you that "the guy who relaxes is helping the Axis. The yard was arranged city-like: F, G, H streets running in one direction, 9th, 10th, 11th streets in another. It was a city without houses, but the traffic was heavy. Cranes, trucks, trains noised by. Finally, after a rather long walk, I came to the edge of the water. There were the ships—or rather, halves, thirds, quarters and tenths of ships. There was a piece of ship here and a piece of ship there, and a hole in between. And then out of a clear blue sky a crane dropped the missing piece of ship, big as a house, into that hole.
—from *Swing Shift* by Joseph Fabry

Thousands of men and women who had never seen a ship before poured into the yard to build Libertys. Shipyard schools were established to train welders, shipfitters, electricians and joiners. By 1943 the number of shipyard workers reached 700,000, as compared to less than 100,000 during the busiest peacetime years. Salesmen, farmers, students—people who might never have been brought together—all swelled the ranks of shipyard workers. Women, too, signed up in great numbers. At one time, they made up more than 30 percent of the work force at the shipyards. Rosie the Riveter became a popular national image, winding up as a Norman Rockwell cover of the *Saturday Evening Post*. Women contributed to all spheres of construction, but most worked as welders, earning themselves another nickname: Wendy the Welder. Women's presence enlivened many work crews, romances flowered and competition between the sexes brought out the best efforts in both. Over 100 Libertys were named after women, both the famous and the little known. There were the *Amelia Earhart*, the *Betsy Ross*, the *Dolley Madison*, the *Pocahontas*, and the *Emma Lazarus*.

The Henry J. Kaiser shipyard in Richmond, California, completed its first Liberty ship in 197 days. In August 1942 the Kaiser yard in Portland, Oregon, turned out the Liberty *Pierre S. DuPont* in 31 days. The Richmond yard then finished the *Joseph W. Teal* in 16 days. But the record effort went to the Kaiser gang that assembled the *Robert E. Peary* in just 4 days, fifteen hours.

Named and freshly painted wartime gray, a Liberty ship still did not take aboard a single bag of grain or round of ammunition until it passed a series of rigid seaworthiness tests. The Maritime Commission's trial board went for a two-day outing with throttles opened wide. A full crew demonstrated the ship's readiness by spinning her wheel on a dizzying course, swinging her in circles, running her astern full speed. All the while trial board members combed the ship from forepeak to poop, listening to her purr, testing her fuel consumption, her horsepower, surveying her holds, inspecting her equipment, pipes, wiring, and safety devices.
—from *Historic Ships of San Francisco* by Steven E. Levingston

At top: On the bridge of the Liberty ship
Jeremiah O'Brien in San Francisco Bay.

83

The Hunted

A full two years before World War Two began, preparations had been put in hand to provide the merchantmen with paravanes (an anti-mine device trailed on the beam), and with deck armament to meet the threat of U-boats. There had been no shortage of volunteers to man the guns, and training courses for them were being run in several British ports. By the end of 1939, 1,500 guns had been mounted on merchant ships, and the vessels' fabric strengthened to support them and withstand their recoil; most of the guns, however, were of World War One vintage, and were only capable of firing at low elevations. There was a serious shortage of weapons for defence against air attack. The few available Lewis light machine-guns had to be switched from ship to ship as one came into port and another sailed. On one occasion, a seaman, furious at the feeling of impotence, hurled a grenade at a low-flying attacking aircraft, and scored a bullseye on its fuselage. It was a brave effort, which could only have been bettered if he had remembered to remove the firing pin.

From the beginning of World War Two, Germany made widespread use of a British invention which dated from the First War. This was the magnetic mine, of which large numbers were "sown" by U-boats in British coastal waters, and by aircraft in harbour mouths and estuaries. Approximately one in every four mines laid caused damage, and many merchant ships were sunk. An Admiralty team had been examining the problem for some time, but it was not until an unexploded mine, dropped by parachute off Shoeburyness in November 1939, was hauled ashore and taken to pieces (with courage and great care) that the appropriate countermeasures were devised. The first, and simplest, was to detonate the mines at a safe distance, but there were not enough mine-sweepers to carry out the task. Another measure was to de-magnetise or "degauss" a ship (gauss being the unit of magnetic induction) by passing an electric current through copper cables wrapped around the hull.

By the spring of 1940, 2,000 merchant ships and 1,704 warships had been degaussed, but there were 10,000 vessels on Lloyd's Register alone, and enormous lengths of cable would have been required had not a Naval Mines Department scientist suggested that the same effect could be achieved by using a temporary coil to pass a very powerful current through the ship, and so neutralise its magnetic field. This process came to be known as "wiping", and the knowledge that his ship had been thoroughly "wiped" convinced the majority of seamen that they were safe, at least from the magnetic mine.

In the early years of the war, few self-respecting Navy men wanted to be assigned to convoy duties, and in the warships' wardrooms, noses were turned up at the very notion of specialising in anti-submarine activity. After all, who would not rather do battle with the *Bismarck* or the *Tirpitz* than trudge across the oceans with a lot of tramps and tankers? One of the few to see a future in it was 1st Lieutenant (later Rear-Admiral) Philip Burnett, who began the war as Lord Louis Mountbatten's No. 1 on the destroyer HMS *Kelly*. Burnett became the chief instructor at the Navy's anti-submarine school and, in 1943, took command of a Canadian escort group at a time when the Royal Canadian Navy was making a substantial impact in the North Atlantic. By then, attitudes were changing. The Battle of the Atlantic took on a certain glamour, and began to offer a fashionable arena. Thereafter, commands in the Western Approaches were eagerly sought after. Able Seaman Thomas Rowe recalls an attack by German aircraft on the coaster *Empire Daffodil* as she sailed up the Channel bound for

Of the approximately 39,000 men who went to sea in the U-boats, 27,491 died in action. A further 5,000 were made prisoners-of-war.

An al fresco lunch is enjoyed by this U-boat crew at their wartime base in France; right: A Merchant Navy captain in a convoy during the Battle of the Atlantic.

the port of London on 9th July 1940. "We were light ship, having discharged our cargo at Plymouth. The sea was calm, and we were sailing alone in brilliant sunshine, when we were suddenly attacked by Me 109s, diving out of the sun. I manned the Holman projector and fired the missiles until our supply ran out. Apart from the machine-gun on the wing of the bridge there was nothing else to hit back with. We managed to avoid the bombs dropped by the aircraft, but the hull was punctured several times by armour-piercing bullets, and the ship began to take in water. We got into Weymouth harbour just as the tide was running out, and settled in the mud. Royal Navy engineers came out and welded metal plates over the lowest holes, which enabled us to sail into harbour on the next full tide and get the repairs completed."

In March 1941, after Field Marshal Erwin Rommel's lightning campaign in Cyrenaica,

Wavell's Eighth Army held Tobruk like a fortress encircled by the enemy, and even that precarious toe-hold on the shore of North Africa would have been impossible but for the supplies and reinforcements brought in by the Merchant Navy. When at last the Afrika Korps took the fortress, it was the merchant ships which played the major part in the evacuation, as it had done after the collapse of Greece in two short weeks, which put 58,000 British troops at risk of death or capture, and when Crete, too, soon fell to the enemy.

On 27th April 1941, the *City of London* weighed anchor in Kalamata Bay with over 3,000 troops aboard, most of them Australian, and set course for Alexandria. That afternoon, a Scottish soldier came on deck, produced the inevitable bagpipes, and commenced the process of putting them in tune. A recumbent Bren gunner propped himself up on an elbow and voiced a protest. "Give me bloody dive-bombing every time," he proclaimed.

From the beginning of April until 20th May 1941, twenty-five British merchantmen, totalling over 140,000 tons, were sunk, most of them by bombing, in the pleasant blue waters of the Mediterranean. For many months, indeed until the Allies were established in Sicily and on the toe of Italy, the Merchant Navy provided the lifeline for the Allied forces in the Middle East.

A Type VII U-boat re-enters the Bay of Biscay after completing a successful patrol in the North Atlantic in 1941.

There were times when a merchantman, alone on the high seas, was caught by a U-boat on patrol. Then, the master had to choose between defiance and surrender. A Type VIIC U-boat, moving on the surface, could make more than seventeen knots, and few cargo ships could equal that. But if the merchantman put up enough of a fight to persuade the U-boat commander to submerge, that cut its speed by more than half, and there might be a chance of making a run for it. Many a rookie gun-crew fought it out with a U-boat's gunners and, at least for a while, gave as good as they got; many a chief engineer screwed down the safety valves and opened up the taps to maintain his top speed plus a little more; many a helmsman spotted the rippling wake of a torpedo, and took effective evasive action; many a radio operator stayed staunchly at his set, tapping out a call for help while the battle raged around him. The sad fact was that, unless a friendly destroyer or aircraft was in range and could answer the call, the U-boat was almost sure to win the fight.

The second time that Thomas Rowe came under fire was in 1942, when the Great Lakes steamer *Fred W. Green*, bound for Freetown from Bermuda, was attacked in the late evening of 31st May. "Shells smashed into the ship, and into our deck cargo of motor vehicles, which exploded when their petrol tanks were hit. I got away on the one remaining lifeboat. The U-boat, *U506*, came alongside, and the commander asked what ship we were, what cargo we were carrying, and where we were bound. I heard later that *U506* was sunk by aircraft."

In 1943, Britain's operational research people examined the relationship between convoy size and losses, and they found that, in 1942 and 43, the larger convoys, of forty ships or more, had suffered lower per centage losses than those of fewer numbers. They also calculated that the length of a big convoy's perimeter did not increase in proportion with its numbers, and that, if six escorts were needed for a forty-ship convoy, seven were sufficient for one of twice the size. There was the additional consideration that an eighty-ship convoy sailing every fortnight could carry the same tonnage of freight as one of forty ships sailing every week. It meant more problems at assembly points, at the ports of loading and discharge, and more grey hairs for the Commodores: more importantly, it meant more cargoes getting through to their destinations.

Next, the escort tactics came under scrutiny. The principles of warfare held good for the sea as much as for the land and for the air, and although "concentration of effort" came high on the list in the early days of the Atlantic battle, it took a while for the Navy to implement the local superiority of force. Captain Frederick 'Johnny' Walker, the champion escort group leader in the North Atlantic, understood this doctrine and practised it with great success. Once the Asdic operator in Walker's sloop HMS *Starling*, or in one of his ships, identified the sonar echo of a U-boat, it was rare for the U-boat to escape. Churchill himself was persuaded that offensive patrols by such groups as "Walker's chicks", as they were known in Liverpool, paid better dividends than simply shepherding the convoys.

A torpedo might strike home with a sickening thud that shook the ship, make a vast explosion and throw up a towering plume of water, but, if it missed the engine room, it might not have dealt a fatal blow. It would make a great hole below the waterline, but that did not mean the ship would sink, at least, not straightaway. A load of good Canadian timber could keep a ship afloat for days, and holes could be blocked to some extent, if not repaired. Ships travelled far, and sometimes reached their destinations (perhaps helped by a towline or two), with all sorts of damage down below. When the *Carsbreck*, for example, sailing with the ill-

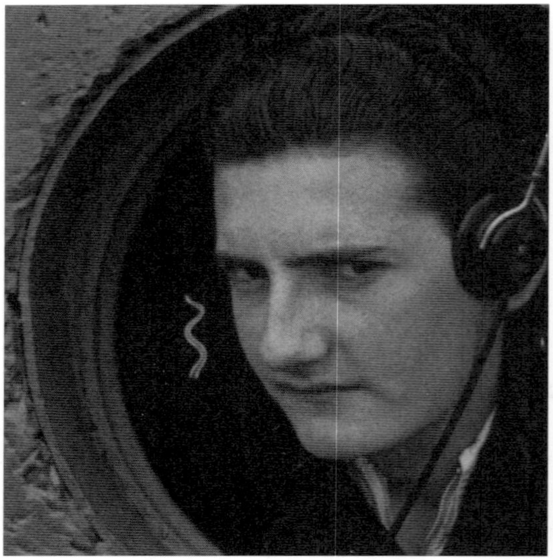

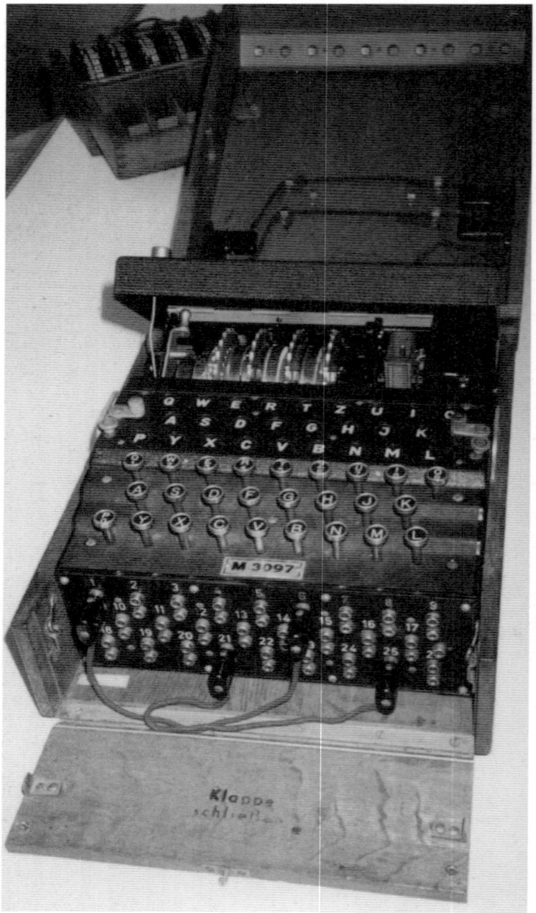
M 3097

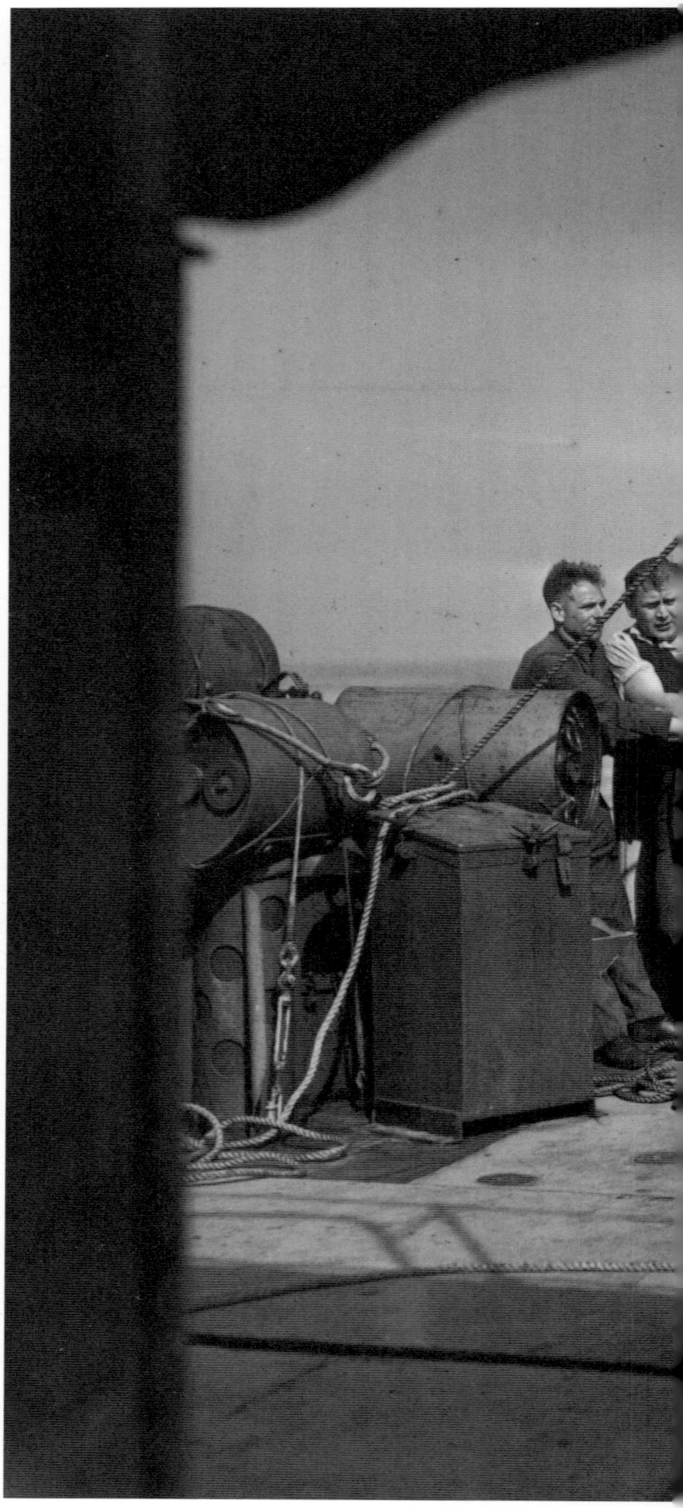

top left: A Merchant Navy wireless operator on duty; bottom left: a German Enigma code cyphering machine, left: a Merchant Navy depth-charge crew on station.

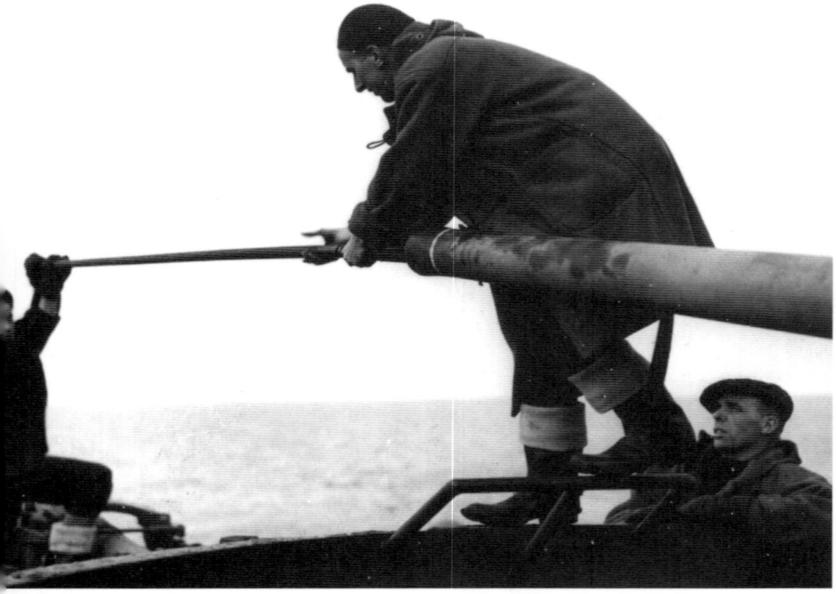

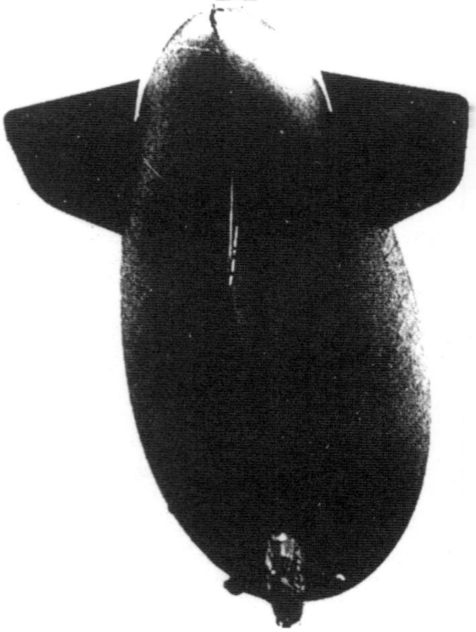

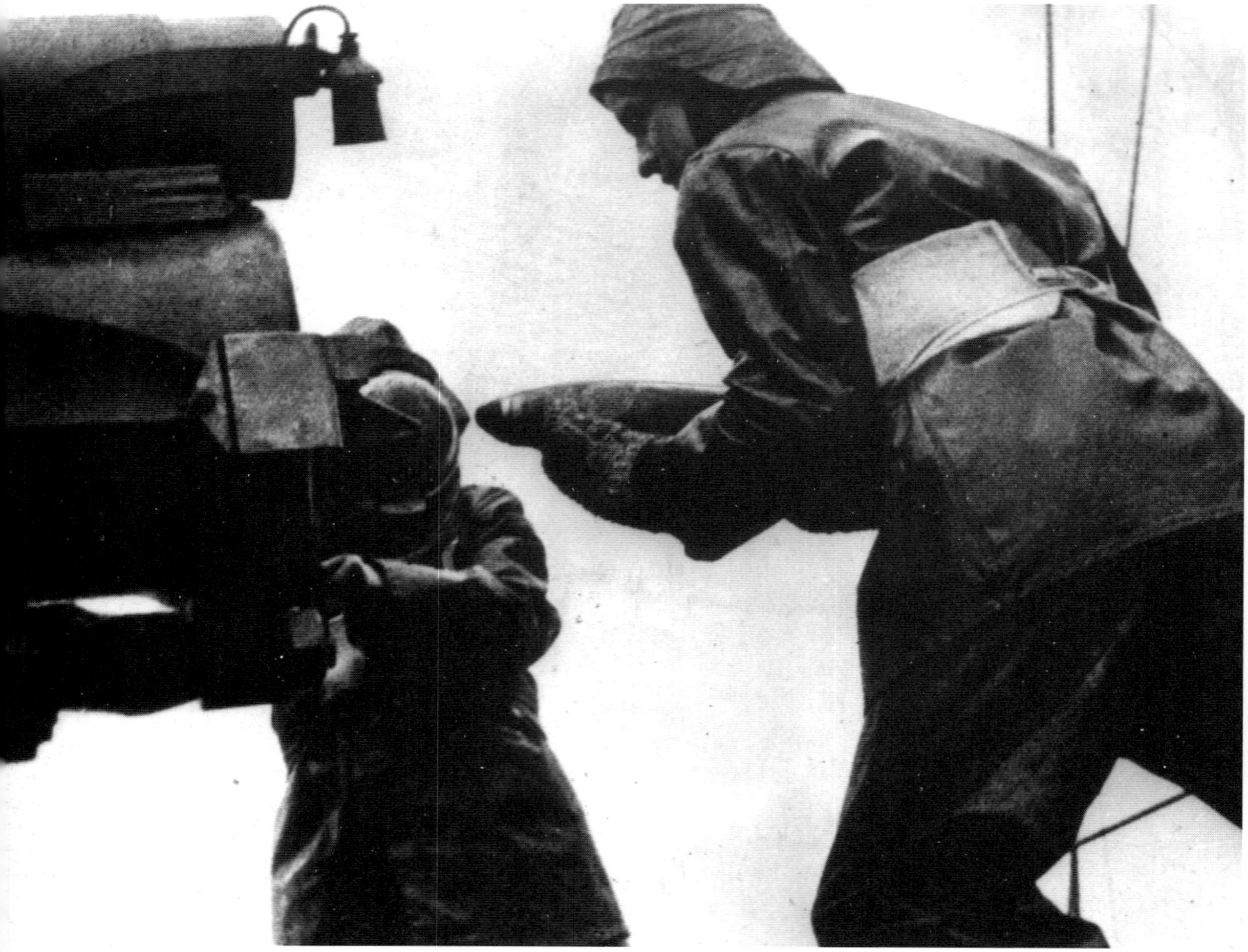

top left: Cleaning the barrel of a deck gun aboard a merchant ship; left and centre: air reconnaissance patrols flown during the Battle of the Atlantic; bottom left: Deck gun loading; below: British warships on escort duty with a Britain-bound convoy early in the Second World War.

U-boat lookouts on convoy duty.

fated convoy SC7 on 17th October 1940, was torpedoed by Heinrich Liebe's *U38*, she went down by the head and listed heavily to port, but her load of timber kept her up, and, steaming at five knots, she struggled on and docked in Liverpool. Sadly, she was one of three ships of convoy HG75 to be sunk by *U564* one year later on 24th October 1941 in the North Atlantic.

Canada's vital contribution to the Battle of the Atlantic was crucial in terms of the administration of the major ports at Halifax, of liaison between Britain and America, of the essential provision of reconnaissance aircraft, escort ships and personnel, and particularly in the construction and operation of corvettes.

There are official charts on which the position of every merchant ship sunk by a U-boat during certain phases of the war is marked by a little cross. For the period April 1940 to March 1941, the crosses stretch from the Faroes, past the southern coast of Ireland, through the Western Approaches (where they lie thick), down past the Spanish coast, the Azores and the western coast of Africa to Freetown. To study such a chart is to feel a shudder of dismay, and to turn to the chart for August 1942 to May 1943 is to be sickened and appalled. By the end of 1943, however, the picture had significantly improved, with the advent of the hunter-killer escort groups, the long-range aircraft with the latest search radar, now operating from the Azores as well as from Britain, Iceland and the Americas. The "air gap" in the Atlantic had been filled, and the losses in November were the lowest since May 1940.

below: An Allied escort vessel; left: A helpful manual for the navy man at sea.

I believe the only time we were really afraid was when the ship's engines broke down and the convoy just sailed on and left us. A ship with no power is like a tomb. There's an unearthly silence, and every hammer blow, every sound of something falling in the engine room, sounds like thunder and makes everyone jump. The ship just lies there, with no leeway, responding to the motion of the sea. Our hearts were in our mouths, knowing how sound, travelling through water, could be picked up by a U-boat. Sometimes we were immobile for twenty-four hours, and there was immense relief when the ship was under way again and belting along at maximum speed to catch up with the convoy and get a 'Welcome back' signal from the Commodore.
—Jack Armstrong, steward, Merchant Navy

When we were somewhere between Port Moresby and Darwin, news came through that the bomb had been dropped on Hiroshima and then on Nagasaki. Early one morning after that, the chap on lookout on the bridge came down into the Mess, woke everybody up, and said the war was over, for which he was abused and accused of pulling our legs. Confirmation of his truthfulness came when he produced a bottle of whisky from the Captain. To get a bottle like that so easy, the war had to be over. As we left Darwin, VJ-Day was declared, and all the ships in harbour were dressed overall, with sirens blowing.
—E. Withers, ex-DEMS gunner, Merchant Navy

From *How To Abandon Ship* by Phil Richards and John J. Banigan: Most casualties at sea are

The various types of depth-charge weapons were intended to destroy or cripple a target submarine through the shock of exploding near it. They were generally dropped by surface ships and later by aircraft and helicopters.

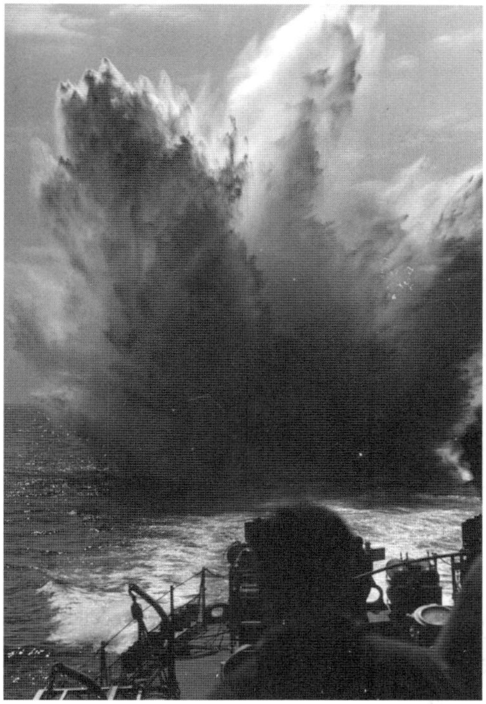

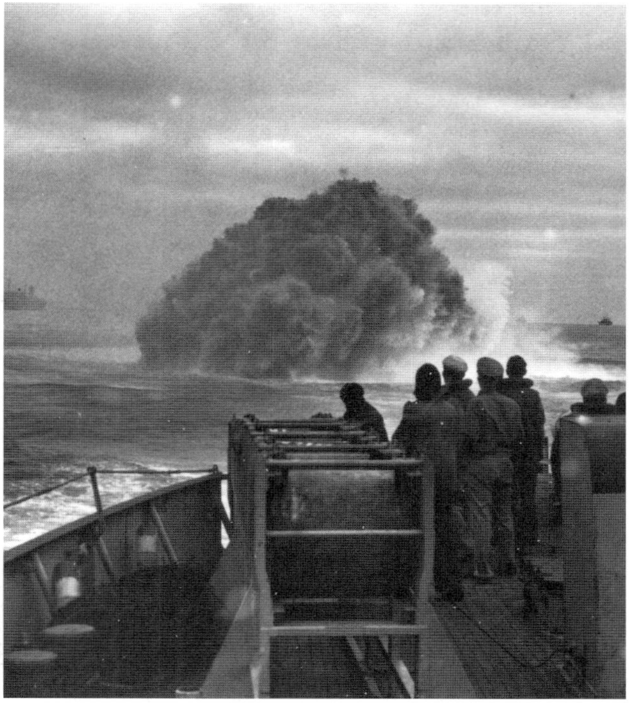

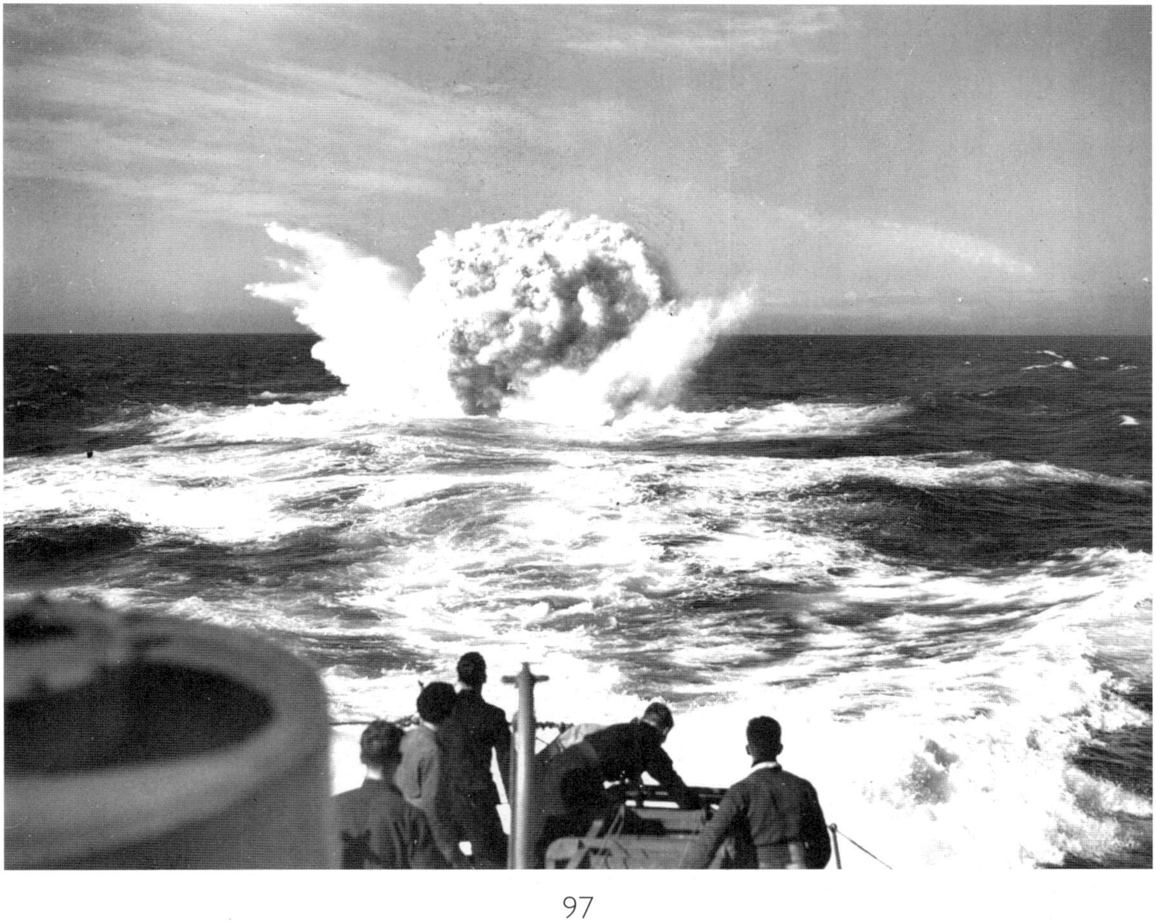

top: A U-boat cook and testing a breathing apparatus; below: Jack Hawkins in a still from the movie *The Cruel Sea*.

actually the result of panic, which is the produce of ignorance. In a life-or-death emergency you are not going to be entirely free of panic. Don't depend on peacetime experience and regulations. Keep your eye out for recent and current bulletins issued by the Marine Inspection Service, which has gathered a large amount of data and from it proposed many improvements and changes in safety and lifeboat regulations. Don't depend on what is in the lifeboat. Don't stint yourself on safety gear for your own protection. Steamship operators are like all other businessmen—except for providing five thousand dollars insurance on each seaman, from the captain to the mess boy. They wish to keep expenses at a minimum. So if the steamship operator does not do the supplying, you yourself do the buying. A few dollars from your pocket may mean all the difference between your becoming a 1943 casualty or a 1983 veteran. Don't let human nature trick you into indifference. A man will readily pay for comfort and a good appearance; but he is reluctant to part with dollars to protect his most precious possession—his own life. The reason for this indifference is plain. He is constantly aware of the benefits of comfort and a good appearance, but death is beyond his experience. He cannot identify himself with it. And death is something that happens to the other fellow.

A great roar went up from the men on the upper deck, a howl of triumph. The U-boat came up bows first at an extraordinary angle, blown right out of her proper trim by the force of the explosion: clearly she was, for the moment, beyond control. The water sluiced and poured from her casings as she rose: great bubbles burst round her conning tower: gouts of oil spread outwards from the crushed plating amidships. "Open fire!" shouted Ericson—and for a few moments it was Baker's chance, and his alone: the two-pounder pom-pom, set just behind the funnel, was the only gun that could be brought to bear. The staccato force of its firing shook the still air, and with a noise and a chain of shock like the punch! punch! punch! of a trip-hammer the red glowing tracer-shells began to chase each other low across the water towards the U-boat. She had now fallen back on a level keel, and for the moment she rode at her proper trim: it was odd, and infinitely disgusting, suddenly to see this wicked object, the loathsome cause of a hundred nights of fear and disaster, so close to them, so innocently exposed. It was like seeing some criminal, who had outraged honour and society, and had long been shunned, taking his ease at one's own fireside.
—from *The Cruel Sea* by Nicholas Monsarrat

During the past 3 1/2 years, the Navy has been dependent upon the Merchant Marine to supply our far-flung fleet and bases. Without this support, the Navy could not have accomplished its mission. Consequently, it is fitting that the Merchant Marine share in our success as it shared in our trials. The Merchant Marine is a strong bulwark of national defense in peace and war, and a buttress to a sound national economy. A large Merchant Marine is not only an important national resource; it is, in being an integral part of the country's armed might during time of crisis. During World War Two, this precept had been proven. As the Merchant Marine returns to its peacetime pursuits, I take pleasure in expressing the Navy's heartfelt thanks to you and through you to the officers and men of the Merchant Marine for their magnificent support during World War Two. All hands can feel the pride of accomplishment in a job well done. We wish the Merchant Marine every success during the years ahead and

sincerely hope that it remains strong and continues as a vital and integral part of our national economy and defense.
—Fleet Admiral Ernest J. King, Commander-in-Chief, United States Navy and Chief of Naval Operations

A pretty young woman asked me if I were interested in meeting and staying with a family for a night. It was such a wonderful opportunity and I agreed without hesitation. I took the address and directions to the home, which was out of the city, and after a short bus ride arrived at their doorstep. They invited me in and served me some tea and biscuits. That evening we enjoyed a delicious but spare dinner of meat pie, potatoes, bread and tea. We then set about talking about the terrible war and the young men "such as yourself" who were involved. I retired for the night in the comfort of their home. In the morning breakfast was ready, consisting of an egg, some toast and marmalade and tea. I bade them goodbye and returned to the ship where I told my shipmates of my evening and of breakfast. "You what?" yelled one of the fellows. "You at their egg! Goddammit, they only get about one egg a month and you ate it. You stupid son of a bitch" I was at a loss and felt so guilty and full of remorse, and yet it was too late to do anything about it.
—Thom Hendrickson, DEMS Signalman, US Navy

The claustrophobic, insanitary, stench-filled and ultimately hellish conditions of living in the narrow drum of a U-boat.

Tanker

Of all the products Britain needed for survival in the 1940s, let alone to fight the war, oil was crucial, and every gallon had to come from overseas, so the role of her tanker fleets, and those of friendly nations, was absolutely vital to the Allied cause. The large peacetime supplies from the East and Middle East had reached Britain through the Suez Canal and the Mediterranean—a route which from June 1940 was virtually closed. Winston Churchill faced the fact that Britain needed the capacity of four large tankers every day: "I trust steps are being taken," he instructed the Secretary for Petroleum, "to draw as much oil as possible from America, thus avoiding the long haul from the Persian Gulf round the Cape.

The tankers *Regent Tiger* and *Kennebec*, sunk by U-boats in the Western Approaches, were two of twenty-five merchant vessels to be lost in the first three weeks of war. From then on, the officers and men of all the major oil carriers—Anglo-Saxon Petroleum (Shell), Anglo-American (Esso), British Oil Tankers, Bulk Oil, Eagle Oil, Northern Petroleum, and Oriental—were in the thick of the Atlantic battle, and they were carrying the most dangerous of cargoes. Ships loaded with wheat, meat and iron might be holed and sunk, might turn over, catch on fire, but they would rarely burn like furnaces until they exploded, turning the sea into a blazing cauldron in which a quick death by drowning was a merciful release.

On 12th August 1940, the 8,000-ton tanker British Fame, sailing with convoy OB193 between Madeira and the Azores, earned the dubious distinction of becoming the first vessel of the war to be sunk by an Italian submarine. The successful *Malaspia* was one of the twenty-seven-strong Atlantic Flotilla which il Duce, Benito Mussolini, had positioned under Admiral Dönitz's command at Bordeaux.

Captain George Waite of Eagle Oil had the worst of luck. It was as though fate had chosen him to meet disaster after disaster. In December 1939, his *San Alberto*, outward bound for Trinidad, had been torpedoed and sunk 140 miles south of Fastnet. Eleven months later, he gave the order to abandon the blazing *San Demetrio* when the *Admiral Scheer* attacked convoy HX84 in the Western Approaches, and the *Jervis Bay* fought to the end, like a mother chicken defending her brood. On 15th June 1943, Waite was to be master of the *San Ernesto*, in ballast for Bahrain from Sydney, when tankers, however, occasionally demonstrated a degree of survivability denied to other ships. The derelict *San Ernesto* drifted for 2,000 miles before she ran aground, and the famous story of the *San Demetrio* epitomises the bravery and endurance of the merchant seamen at war. Her crew, too, had engaged the *Admiral Scheer* with their only gun, but it was a hopeless gesture. While star-shells lit the evening sky, two shots from the *Scheer*'s big guns hit the tanker. Her flying bridge was broken, her navigation bridge a mass of tangled iron, her bows and well-decks were holed, there was damage in her boiler room and engine room, and she was ablaze Captain Waite put his confidential papers in a weighted bag and threw it overboard, and all but three of her crew got clear in the lifeboats, which lost contact in the night with each other and with the *San Demetrio*. The sixteen men in one lifeboat saw the Swedish steamer *Stureholm* in the distance, picking up survivors from the *Jervis Bay*, and tried but failed to catch the rescuer's attention.

Taking turns at the oars, they rowed the lifeboat for two days in rain and heavy seas, but such were the winds and motion of the waves that, on the second day, they found themselves still in sight of the tanker, which was afire and pouring smoke. They pulled toward her, and there was some discussion as to whether they should board her (she was carrying 11,200 tons of petrol). It was an American apprentice seaman, Oswald Preston, known to the crew as "Yank", who decided the issue when he said that he would rather fry than freeze. Later, he described what happened when the tanker was re-boarded: "We were appalled by the spectacle, but we set to work to put out the fires on the deck where the petrol was forcing its way out through the shrapnel holes. All but one of the hoses were burnt, and we had to work with buckets of water from the sea. Chief Pollard, with George Willey, the third engineer, and John Boyle, a greaser, made their way down to the engine room through three feet of water, and got the pumps going, which meant we could use the hose to fight the fires. It took eleven hours before we got them under control, Somehow, the engineers got steam up, and the ship was under way."

The question then was which way they should go? Westward would be safer, but against the wind and weather; eastward lay their destination in the Clyde, but also the enemy's U-boats and aircraft. There was another brief discussion. "We've come this far with the petrol," was the general opinion. "Let's finish the job." A system of lights was rigged up to pass the signals from what was left of the bridge to the engine room. Chief Engineer Pollard wrote on his log: "9th Nov. Resumed passage." Next day, John Boyle died from internal injuries, aggravated by exposure in the lifeboat. The engines were stopped, and his body was committed to the deep.

The next problem was how to navigate the tanker. The wireless, charts, and instruments had gone, the compass was showing a massive deviation (the effect of all the broken metal on the ship) and the main steering gear was broken. All 2nd Officer Hawkins had to work with was the sun by day, the stars by night, and a six-penny atlas. "We ought to make a landfall," said Hawkins, "somewhere between Narvik and Gibraltar." In fact, he found Clew Bay on the west coast of Ireland eight days after the *San Demetrio* had been reported lost, and she continued her voyage to Rothesay in the Firth of Clyde where, at the crew's insistence, her own pumps and pipes were used to discharge some 3,000,000 gallons of precious gasoline. Captain Waite, meanwhile, and the remaining twenty-two members of the crew, had been taken aboard the SS *Gloucester City* and landed at St Johns, Newfoundland on the 12th of November.

When Chief Pollard and others were honoured at a lunch in London, he paid a tribute to the *Jervis Bay*'s crew: "While we have such men as those guarding our convoys and waterways, we shall not go hungry." Some of those who heard him added in their hearts: "And with such men as these to sail our tankers, we shall not go short of fuel."

Charles Pollard and George Willey were awarded a very special medal—Lloyd's Medal for Bravery at Sea. Pollard also received the OBE, and they all shared in the £14,700 salvage money that Eagle Oil paid out to the crew. They wanted "Yank" Preston to have the *San Demetrio*'s tattered Red Ensign, but he could not be found, and the flag remains in the London office of the company to this day.

"British tanker makes a great film story," was the headline in the Sunday Express when the Ealing Studios film "San Demetrio" was shown in January 1944, and the review ended ". . . the most satisfying fact, which sailors will appreciate, is that the director has avoided every temptation to glamourise the story. For once, it is a report on what happened. It goes into the class of true life dramas . . . an authentic thriller of the times."

In the early hours of 3rd April 1941, the twenty-two ships of convoy SC26 were in the mid-Atlantic gap, beyond the point at which the Canadian escort had left them, not yet at the point where the escort from the UK was to meet them, and with only an armed merchant cruiser to protect them. Admiral Dönitz could not have picked a better moment for his wolfpack to attack. The *British Viscount*, carrying 10,000 tons of fuel oil, was one of several tankers in the convoy, and William Reuben Virgo Bourner was her 2nd Engineer. What follows is his story of the attack and of its aftermath: "The *British Viscount* was an old steam turbine ship, and we had been having trouble with the auxiliaries, so we had two engineers working six-hour watches. The U-boat attacks started at about 10:30 in the evening of 2nd April, and the the first to be sunk was another of our company's tankers, the *British Reliance*. Then a Belgian ship with a cargo of iron ore, was almost abeam of us when it was torpedoed and sank instantly. From then on, ships were sunk at the rate of roughly one an hour.

"No increase in speed was ordered until about 3:15 a.m. when, hearing the engine telegraph ringing, I went below to order the men to open the extra nozzles on the turbines. A few moments later, we heard a terrible grinding sound above the noise of the turbines, and the ship heeled over twenty degrees. I shouted to the 3rd Engineer to stop, while I opened the astern valve to bring the ship to a stop as soon as possible. The 3rd Engineer and I shut the master valve to the boiler oil pumps as we went aloft. There had been no messages from the bridge during this time, and when we reached the boat deck I could see why: the ship was a mass of flame, and the fire was rapidly spreading aft.

"One lifeboat was in the water, and we slid down the ropes and climbed aboard. We had some difficulty in getting the boat's bow round, as the crew had dropped it on the weather

The tanker *San Demetrio* was attacked and set ablaze by German raiders. She was saved by the heroic efforts of Chief Engineer Charles Pollard and other crew members.

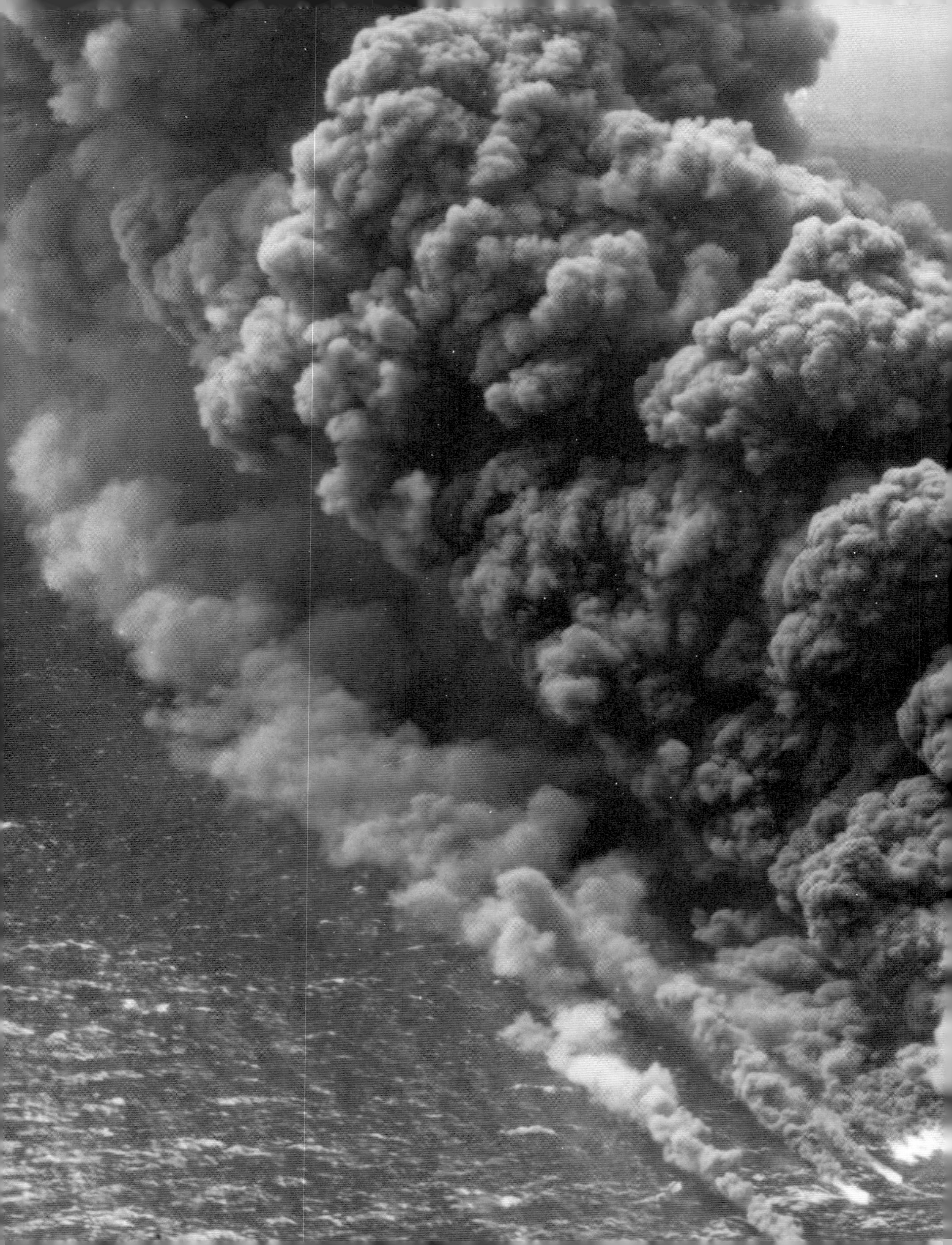

The demise of a blazing Allied oil tanker torpedoed by a German submarine in the North Atlantic.

A useful guide for mariners in wartime.

side, but that proved to be lucky because, by the time we got it away from the tanker, the oil was burning on the water and it was getting pretty warm. Just as we were pushing off, a cabin boy managed to get out of a port-hole amidships, and we were just in time to catch him as he floated by. By then, the *British Viscount* was a blazing inferno.

"About three hours later, we found one of our firemen on a small raft, and pulled him on board—with some difficulty because the waves were six or seven feet high. That made twenty of us in the lifeboat, out of a crew of forty-eight. We had lost the captain, three deck officers, the radio officer, chief steward, engine room crew, carpenter and sailors. We had a senior apprentice in the boat, who said that the nearest land was Greenland, about 200 miles away, and we decided we would have a better chance of being sighted from a rescue ship if we stayed near the tanker, which by now was just a hulk.

"After about twelve hours, a destroyer, HMS *Havoc*, [probably *Havelock*, author], came into view and picked us up. And very good to us, they were, too. More survivors were picked up during the next few hours, which brought the total up to seventy. Another destroyer was also in the area, picking up survivors. We heard later that we had lost ten ships that night—nearly half the convoy. At least, the Navy got one of them: two days later, our destroyer made full speed for twenty minutes or so, and came to two corvettes, with a U-boat close by, which then turned turtle and sank as we watched. One of the corvettes lowered a boat to pick up the crew."

In September 1941, the 12,842-ton *San Florentino*, another Eagle Oil ship, twenty-two years old, sailing in ballast from the Clyde, quit the convoy after leaving port, and proceeded on her route to Curacao, off the coast of Venezuela, where she was to load with gasoline. On 27th September, she was sighted through the periscope of *U94*, and shadowed for two days. As night fell on the second day, an epic fight began, which lasted for two hours, the tanker taking evasive action, and returning fire with her 4.7-inch gun. At last, she was hit with torpedoes, first on the starboard beam and then on the port. With the tanker badly damaged and listing heavily to port, Captain Davis and his crew fought on, and holed the U-boat's conning tower. Then, the tanker was hit again, and a fourth torpedo struck the death blow. She was holed amidships, the whole breadth of the vessel, and began to break in two.

The *San Florentino* went down some 900 miles east of Newfoundland, but her fore part stayed afloat, grotesquely vertical, with the stern protruding a hundred feet into the air. Third Officer Todd and Able Seaman Clayton climbed up, and sat astride the bow for thirteen hours, until they were rescued by HMCS *Mayflower*. The gun crew, meanwhile, had managed to launch an undamaged lifeboat, but another, the starboard midship boat, was stove in and only just afloat, with its gunwales under water. Sitting waist deep in this and in a bitter wind, nine of the nineteen men aboard died of cold and exposure in the eleven hours that passed before the boat was found. Captain Davis and twelve members of his gallant crew went down with the *San Florentino*. The next month, October 1941, six more tankers were sunk by U-boats and another damaged.

"What you have to remember," said a tanker sailor, "is that she's in ballast half the time, with water in her tanks, and then she's the safest ship afloat.". When a tanker was loaded, however, there was very little freeboard, and even a moderate sea would wash across the decks. Another tanker man remembers an Atlantic crossing when a northerly gale and a heavy sea between them swept away the lifeboat and davits on the weather side.

When the *San Vulfrano* was being loaded with aviation spirit for the RAF in Britain, crewman Thomas Rowe overheard a longshoreman say, "If they get hit with that load aboard, the crew won't need life jackets to keep them up—they'll need parachutes to bring them down."

The heat from a burning tanker could be felt at a range of 1,500 yards, and the fire could go on burning for six hours. At other times, a stricken tanker might erupt like a volcano and be gone in the twinkling of an eye. That was what happened to the 8,000-ton *San Victorio* off the coast of Venezuela on 17th May 1942. She was on her maiden voyage, full of aviation

The lookouts aboard a Type VII U-boat in the Battle of the Atlantic.

petrol from Aruba Island, when she was hit by a torpedo from *U155* and immediately caught fire. Two vast explosions followed. The first blew gunner Anthony Ryan, who was standing on the poop, over the stern rail and far into the sea. Somehow, this sturdy man kept afloat for sixteen hours, without a lifebelt or any form of raft, in a sea full of sharks and barracuda. He was the sole survivor of the *San Victorio*.

All in all, the first eight months of 1942 were a bad time for tankers, especially for those of Eagle Oil, who lost seven, with 269 officers and men, mostly off America's east coast or in the Caribbean Sea. Indeed, they were not good months for in the Merchant Navy or the Merchant Marine. "Milch Cow" submarines, replacing the supply ships, were replenishing the raiders' fuel, provisions and torpedoes, and keeping them at sea for much longer than before. There were more big Type IX U-boats, more reliable torpedoes, and a lot more young Kapitänleutnants, all determined to make their names as aces, now that Günther Prien and Joachim Schepke had gone down and Otto Kretschmer was a prisoner-of-war.

It was the American "industrial miracle" which gave a silver lining to the dark clouds of the year. Although the great advances in ship production had not yet been reflected in the tanker fleet (the sixty-two built in 1942 did not make up for the losses), by the end of May 1943, production had been stepped up to fourteen or fifteen a month and, for the first time, U-boat sinkings were exceeded by new ships. The T-2, which was typical, was 523.5 feet long, had a beam of sixty-eight feet, a draught when loaded of nearly thirty feet, turbo-electric power, a speed of more than fourteen knots, and a dead weight of 16,165 tons. The T-3 was a little bigger, with a dead weight of 18,302 tons, and a speed of eighteen knots.

There was, however, no respite for the tankers in the early months of 1943. Convoy TM1 sailed from Trinidad for North Africa on 28th December 1942, with nine tankers carrying fuel oil and other military stores. Operation Torch had been a brilliant success, but now the Allied armies and air forces were trying to drive Rommel's Afrika Korps out of Tunisia and bring the campaign to an end. They needed fuel for their tanks, trucks, aircraft and coastal craft, and TM1's tankers were bringing twenty-five million gallons of it. The convoy was accompanied by a Royal Navy escort group consisting of the destroyer HMS *Havelock* and three Flower Class corvettes. There would be air cover from America for the first day.

The convoy formed three columns, with the ninth ship sailing on the starboard wing. Six hours out from Trinidad, a report came from a patrolling Catalina flying boat of a U-boat sighting some few miles ahead. *Godetia*, one of the corvettes, hurried to the reported spot and, more in hope than anger, dropped a pattern of depth-charges. The next three days were peaceful, but the convoy had been sighted from *U514*, en route back to base from the Caribbean. The convoy's course, speed and position were radioed to Lorient, and Admiral Dönitz ordered six U-boats, lying between Madeira and the Azores, to sail south at their best speed and intercept. The *U514*, meanwhile, was instructed to shadow the convoy but Kapitänleutnant Auffermann did more than that. In the early evening, he torpedoed *British Vigilance*, leading the centre column, and her voyage ended in one vast explosion.

In the wheel-house of the *Empire Lytton*, immediately astern, Captain Andrews turned hard to starboard to avoid the burning hulk of the *British Vigilance*. Then, in silhouette against the flames, he saw the U-boat lying on the surface, and an avenging instinct made him swing the wheel again to ram. Smoothly, *U514* slid away beneath his bows, but not before a young apprentice, leaping to an Oerlikon, had scored hits on the conning tower with an accurate burst of 20mm shells. When the tanker *Narvik* joined in with a few rounds from her four-inch guns, Auffermann submerged, but continued following the convoy. Two hours later, the *Empire Lytton* caught up with the convoy and took the *British Vigilance*'s station in the lead. But now the escort ships were running low on fuel, and when an attempt was made to refuel from the *Narvik*, which carried the necessary pipelines, the seas were too rough to carry out the transfer. The escort commander ordered a northward change of course for calmer water, and that could not have suited the waiting U-boats better, *U381* sighted the convoy, some 600 miles to the west of the Canaries, in the afternoon of 8th January 1943.

The escort ships were having further problems: HMS *Havelock*'s HFDF was operating intermittently, and two of the corvettes had unserviceable radars. When the wolfpack attacked in the evening, the *British Oltenia II* was sunk and the Norwegian *Albert L. Ellsworth* was set on fire. The assault continued throughout the night, and the *Minister Wedel* and the *Narvik* were both hit by torpedoes but did not catch fire. The escort struggled to protect the remaining tankers. In the early morning hours of 9th January, two torpedoes from *U442* hit the *Empire Lytton* on the starboard bow, and Captain Andrews knew that his ship could become a furnace within minutes, as the *British Vigilance* had done. There was no fire. The stem was holed, however, and the ship was making water. Andrews decided his best course was to abandon her, and lie off in the lifeboats until dawn. The decks, davits, and falls were smothered with thick, black oil from the ruptured forward fuel tanks, and the launching in the darkness turned into a nightmare. One boat was never found, most men took a soaking, and the Chief Officer was drowned.

When Andrews re-boarded the tanker in the morning of 9th January, with thirty-one survivors from his crew of forty-seven, he was at once faced with an order from the escort com-

above: The wireless operator in a U-boat of WW2; right: Painting 'victory' pennants of shipping sunk on patrol.

mander: if the *Empire Lytton* could not get under way and make eight knots, she must be abandoned and would be sunk by gunfire. As the Chief Engineer could promise nothing better than six knots, she was abandoned once again. From the bridge of the corvette HMS *Saxifrage*, Andrews saw a flash and a column of black smoke on the horizon and, saddened, turned away. *Havelock*'s guns, however, had not sunk her: five hours later, she was still afloat when Korvettenkapitän Hesse, returning in *U44*, fired his last torpedo into her.

Meanwhile, the stricken *Narvik* and *Minister Wedel* had gone down, and the *Albert L. Ellsworth* had been finished off by *U436*. By nightfall on 9th January, only three of TM1's tankers were afloat, and the wolfpack had not finished yet. In the evening of 10th January, four U-boats slipped between the escorts on the surface and launched their attacks. The *British Dominion* was hit, and blew up with her load of avgas. Only the *Vanja* and the *Cliona*, watched over by a Catalina and with three more warships in their escort, reached North Africa—the sole survivors of convoy TM1.

After the Allied armies had gone ashore in Normandy, and were advancing into France, they too, needed vast quantities of fuel to keep them on the move. The preparation for Pluto (pipeline under the ocean) had long been in hand and, in July 1944, a pipeline was laid from the Isle of Wight to Cherbourg. Before Pluto came on stream, a fleet of tankers, known as the Hamble Circus, carried fuel from the Solent to the invasion beaches and later to the liberated Channel ports. When the big motor tanker *Empire Russell* carried a million gallons into Cherbourg on 27th June, she was the first Allied merchant ship to enter a north European port for more than four years.

Kapitänleutnant Gerd Schreiber of *U-95* in Saint Nazaire, France, March 1941.

I enjoyed being on tankers. The conditions were better than on the freighters, and so was the food. The downside was that we were berthed at oil installations, well away from town and city centres, and when we got to port, discharge only took a day. But when we had the chance, we lived life to the full, and our motto was 'Live each day as though it were your last.'
—Jack Armstrong, tanker steward, Merchant Navy

Swim, wounded and bomb-shocked, through flaming oil which clogs throat and nostrils and scorches everything it touches, to a bullet-riddled boat. In that very precarious refuge, whilst an equally dazed and damaged shipmate scoops the viscous filth from your breathing passages, watch the ship you have fought through thousands of leagues of danger—man-made and elemental—break apart and plunge sullenly to the bottom of the sea it has gallantly defied for years. Remember, as you play spectator to such a shameful tragedy, that in all probability, your best friends lie mangled and dead among the twisted wreckage. These dead men cheered you on when the battle for existence seemed too fierce to allow of any hope. They taught you the trade of the sea, and showed you the sea's mysteries and immensities.
—from The Merchant Navy at War by Captain Frank H. Shaw

From How to Abandon Ship by Phil Richards and John J. Banigan: "You should provide a means to open the potato locker quickly. Get a sack of potatoes in your lifeboat, and a sack of onions, if possible, or turnips. Because of their high water content, these vegetables will serve double purpose in your rations. Canned tomatoes are important. Do not pass up the bottles of jam. The sugar in them will provide energy. If possible, set your watch to Greenwich time. The mate in your boat may not have a chance to set his watch. He will not be able to calculate longitude with any accuracy without Greenwich time when taking sights. If time permits, get two or three of the rockets which are stowed on the bridge. Be sure your lifeboat is equipped with a flare pistol. Take a roll of toilet paper with you. A Mason jar will keep your matches and other small items dry. Night puts an added burden on you and you must take extra precautions, because at night there is sure to be more panic than in the daytime."

You have seen him on the street, rolling round on groggy feet, / You have seen him clutch a lamp post for support. / You have seen him arm in arm with a maid of doubtful charm / Who was leading Johnny safely back to port. / You have shuddered in disgust as he sometimes bites the dust. / You've ignored him when you've seen him on a spree. / But you've never seen the rip of his dark and lonely ship / Ploughing furrows through a sub-infested sea. / You have cheered our naval lads in their stately iron-clads, / You have spared a cheer for infantry men too. / You have shuddered in a funk when you read 'Big mail boat sunk', / Did you ever give a thought about the crew? / Yet he brings the wounded home through a mine-infested zone And he ferries all the troops across at night. / He belongs to no brigade, he's neglected, underpaid, / But he's always in the thickest of the fight. / And he fights the lurking Hun with his ancient four-inch gun / And he'll ruin Adolf Hitler's little plan. / He's a hero, he's a nut, he's the bloody limit—but, / He's just another Merchant Navy man.—anon

The freedom of the seas is the *sine qua non* of peace, equality and co-operation.
—from an address to the United States Senate, 22nd January 1917, by President Woodrow Wilson.

A Cadet's Story

The sea called to Peter Guy when he was still a boy at school, and he answered the call as soon as he was old enough—on his sixteenth birthday. He remained a seaman for the next six years and, as it happened, they were the epic years of the Merchant Navy's history. Peter was accepted as a cadet by Lamport & Holt in December 1939.

"My first ship was the *Balfe*, and we sailed from Liverpool for the River Plate on 12th January 1940. That winter was severe and we had barely cleared the Mersey before we ran into a blizzard which lasted some days. It didn't take me long to be seasick, but I still had my watch to keep—four hours on, eight hours off and four hours off and so on. I didn't know what I was doing, or what I was supposed to do, but I knew I was cold, wet and miserable. I remember leaving footprints on the snow-covered deck, and with frequent diversions to the side, when I had to go aft to read the log. But I gradually began to get the hang of things, and apart from being sent down to the engine room for the key to the fog locker, and asking the carpenter for a left-handed hammer, I became accepted and started to learn my trade.

"*Balfe* was a happy ship with a good master and crew, and in spite of her age (she was built in 1919), a very good sea boat, as she was to prove some years later. The carpenter was Norwegian and he gave me two good pieces of advice: get all your drinking and hell-raising done by the age of twenty-one, and always buy the first round when ashore with your shipmates—everyone remembers who bought the first round, but by the fifth or sixth memories begin to be unreliable. He also advised me never to argue with a woman or a wire rope, and how right he was.

"Cadets were considered to be the lowest form of marine life, and cheap labour to boot at fifteen shillings (75p) per month. All the dirty and unwanted jobs fell to the cadets, but you learned to be a good seaman, and when you became an officer there was no job you would tell a sailor to do that your couldn't do as well, if not better. It was hard work, and sometimes dangerous, and even without overtime we could clock up to seventy hours a week. Entering and leaving port could result in a twelve to sixteen hour day.

"Our first port was Montevideo, with the *Graf Spee* and her supply ship *Tacoma* very visible. It was strange to see German sailors close up. Then we crossed the estuary of the River Plate to Buenos Aires where, as we had explosives in our cargo, we lay out in the Roads and discharged them into lighters, for which we were paid extra—a welcome addition to the funds, as sixpence (2.5p) a day didn't buy much ashore, even in those days. Argentina was largely pro-German, but we had invitations to various clubs, and at one they had a barbeque where whole oxen and sheep were roasted in trenches.

"I was on cargo watching one night, keeping an eye on the stevedores to prevent them broaching the cargo, when one of the firemen came weaving down the quayside. He had been imbibing the local fire-water made from wheat, and as he approached the ship he started hitting the iron bollards, daring them to get up and fight fairly, until his hands were a bloody mess. We got him on board and put him to bed, apparently feeling no pain.

"After completing discharge, we set off for Rosario, some 200 miles up the river, where I was introduced to cleaning the bilges (known as bilge-diving); they contained a heady mixture of stinking, stagnant water in which floated putrid and fermenting grain, dead rats and I

Merchant sailor Peter Guy
in World War Two

didn't like to think what else. After a heavy night ashore it was a chastening experience. We loaded a full cargo of bulk and bagged grain and returned safely to Liverpool.

"Another job for the cadets was in the chain locker when the anchor was being raised. The locker was steep, narrow, and slippery, right up to the bows—icy in winter and a sweatbox in the tropics. You were showered with mud and sea water every time. Nevertheless, I enjoyed my first voyage, and was a very different person from the lad who had set off some three months before.

"I rejoined *Balfe* after leave, and we sailed to Southampton, which was to be our base for supplying the British Expeditionary Force in France. Our first trip was to Brest, where we unloaded guns, motor transport and all sorts of supplies, and then returned to Southampton, whence we set off again to take our part in the evacuation of Dunkirk. We were either too slow or too late for that, and we were redirected to Cherbourg, where we were convinced that most of the trucks and guns to be brought back were what we had recently discharged at Brest. We loaded as much as possible, but lost the use of the derricks when the soldiers

left: The torpedoing of a merchantman in the Battle of the Atlantic; below: A U-boat lookout on the high seas; bottom: An Allied convoy under escort bound for Britain.

hauled on both the heavy-lift guys at the same time, buckled the foremast and put all the cargo gear out of action. We took as many troops on board as we could, and most of them were tired, dispirited and beaten for the moment. They sat or lay down wherever they could, few with any arms or equipment, and we did the best we could for them.

"It was at that time we 'won' a Bren gun, which made us the best-armed ship in our flotilla. Until then, our armament had consisted of two Martini Ross .303 rifles, so the Bren, mounted on 'Monkey Island', more than doubled our firepower. There were some weird and wonderful ideas on defences early in the war, because of the shortage of weapons. The first 'funny' I met was the Holman projector, which consisted of a length of pipe connected by a foot pedal to a compressed air cylinder. A hand grenade, with pin removed, was put into a tin which just accommodated it and dropped down the pipe. By guess and by God, the pedal was pressed to send the lot flying upwards, with the tin dropping off and the grenade continuing its flight to explode right in front of the aeroplane and bring it down. However, nobody had thought of putting a gauge on the cylinder to show when the pressure was low, with the result that the tin and grenade would just plop out on the deck, leading to a very hasty exit by all concerned.

"An equally daft idea consisted of two rockets, one on each wing of the bridge, connected by a wire with a parachute attached to each. When a plane approached, the rockets would be fired, the parachutes would open at the correct height, with the wire between them and the plane would obligingly fly into it. There were a few problems: it was impossible to get the rockets to fire at precisely the same time, or to maintain the same rate of climb, even if the wire didn't get snagged in the process. If you got that right, however, and the wire did its job, the liklihood was that the plane would crash onto the ship.

"Things got better as the war progressed, and it was quite common to find a ship with a venerable twelve-pounder anti-aircraft gun and a four-inch anti-sub gun of even older vintage. The twelve-pounder had a circular steel emplacement as a protection against strafing, with a high point forward to prevent us shooting up the bridge in an excess of enthusiasm. It was pretty useless, because it took so long to correct the fuse setting and load again after the first shot that the plane was miles away. So we got an improvement: a projector with two rockets on rails that were fired simultaneously by bringing the terminals of a torch battery together. We were all looking forward to seeing it fired, and the great day came when the convoy had dispersed and we were proceeding independently. The gunner, a retired RN Petty Officer, lined everything up, and told us to stand clear while he pressed the terminals together. There was a short period after the rocket ignited, and then whizzed around in a fiery circle. He staggered out of the emplacement with beard and hair singed, and expressed his feelings in a very forceful and moving way. It was most illuminating, in more ways than one.

"*Balfe*'s next assignment was to take some 2,000 French servicemen, who didn't want to serve under de Gaulle, to Casablanca, whence they could return to Vichy France. The 'tween decks were made into temporary sleeping/living quarters, and wooden lavatories and cook houses were built on deck. The Germans were in control of the western coast of France, so a long detour into the Atlantic was necessary. We weren't exactly sympathetic to what the French were doing, and our feelings about them were heartily reciprocated (nothing changes). All went well, however; we duly left the French in Casablanca and got away to Gibraltar. That was a strange place then. Nobody knew if Spain would come in on Germany's side, and invade the Rock. It was decided that women and children, plus males under sixteen

Merchant Navy gun crews on convoy duty..

and over sixty, were to be evacuated. All merchant ships were pressed into service and we, in view of our previous mission, were well placed to help. We took 500 or so on board and off we went. All went well, and we even had a baby on board, safely delivered by the Chief Steward, once he had drunk enough whisky to steady his nerves. The baby was named after the Captain and the ship, so somewhere there is a Gibraltarian proudly named Alfred Balfe. We rounded Ireland and delivered our cargo to Swansea. I often wondered what happened to them.

"We paid off in the Bristol Channel, and after home leave I joined the *Lassell*. Alfred Bibby was the master, and Johansen was the carpenter—both from my first voyage in *Balfe*. *Lassell* was a lovely ship to sail in, though heavy work on deck (with six hatches served by lattice derricks). She was a twin-screw motor ship, very good in a seaway but difficult to steer, especially in confined waters. We once timed how long it took for the tiller arm to move after the wheel on the bridge was turned, and it was several seconds. A by-product of the steering problem was that one of the cadets (usually me) was put on the wheel when entering or leaving port, which could mean up to six hours of concentrated attention."

Guy's first voyage in *Lassell* was to Bahia, Rio de Janiero and Santos in Brazil, and then, after bunkering in Trinidad, to Boston, Massachusetts. He arrived in time to join the throng in Scollay Square, where everyone was singing, kissing, hugging and seeing in the New Year 1941 in true US fashion. Celebrations over, *Lassell* sailed for Halifax, via the Cape Cod Canal, and, with the convoy Commodore aboard, made the slow journey to Liverpool. It was during an otherwise uneventful trip that one more typical cadet job came Guy's way. It was not too difficult to chip the ice off the officer's toilet outlet while dangling in a bosun's chair: the trick was to rig the chair in such a way that the flood missed him when the blockage was removed.

Lassell sailed for South America again on 5th April 1941, with a mixed bulk cargo and a prize bull, destined for breeding in Argentina, penned up on the deck. After a few days, the convoy dispersed, and Captain Bibby headed south, zig-zagging in the daylight until the weather worsened. At six o'clock in the evening on 30th April, some 300 miles southwest of the Cape Verdes, Cadet Guy had just completed a two-hour wheel watch, and was looking forward to his dinner, when there was what he described as "an almighty bang". Picking himself up off the deck, he ran to his allotted lifeboat, No. 2, which was on the weather side. The ship was still under way, and the boat was dashed against the side and badly damaged. Cooly, Guy visited his cabin, collected his wallet and a few possessions, and returned to the boat deck to assist in launching the No. 3 lifeboat.

The torpedo, launched from a Type IXB U-boat, *U107*, had struck *Lassell* on the port side in the engine room near No. 4 bulkhead. Both engines had stopped, the engine room was flooded, the radio was put out of action, and No. 4 lifeboat was smashed. By ten minutes past six, *Lassell* was settling by the stern as the two remaining lifeboats pulled away. They were followed by a quantity of flotsam, several life rafts, and the bull. Captain Bibby took charge of No. 1 boat, with the 1st and 2nd Officers, twenty-six men and a lady passenger, while Chief Underhill, in charge of No. 3 boat, had Guy and another nineteen men on board. An engineer and a greaser were missing and they were assumed to have been trapped in the engine room and drowned.

Five minutes later the U-boat surfaced some 300 yards away from the lifeboats, and members of the crew put an end to the struggles of the bull with their machine-gun. Then the

Lifeboats and rescues at sea during the Atlantic battle.

The other enemy of the seamen of both sides, the weather.

U-boat disappeared. In his war diary, Kapitänleutnant Günther Hessler wrote: "Good shot in engine room, large white blast column, ship lists immediately fifteen degrees to port, and sinks deeper at the stern. A few seconds after the sinking violent underwater explosions are heard in the submarine."

Lassell was Hessler's sixth victim since he set out from Lorient on 29th March. *U107* was resupplied at sea, and sank another eight merchantmen off the west coast of Africa before completing its patrol, of which, in his memoirs, Admiral Dönitz wrote: "He sank fourteen ships with a total tonnage of 87,000—a remarkable performance. He had already done well on his previous operational tour, and with this recent success added, he had gone well past the success mark at which the award of the Knight's Cross was normally made. However, I found it a little difficult to recommend him, because he was my son-in-law. Eventually the Commander-in-Chief put an end to my hesitations by telling me that if I did not recommend Hessler at once, he would."

As Hessler continued on his deadly way, the men in the lifeboats began to organise themselves. The stores on the wrecked No. 2 boat were removed to No. 3, and Nos. 1 and 3 were balanced by transferring five members of the crew. The radio officer broadcast their position every hour on the portable set. At six o'clock in the evening of the second day, a large steamer was sighted, travelling north some four miles to the east. Despite more broadcasts and two distress flares, it continued on its course—a disappointment which was to be repeated several times.

Next morning a seven-gallon water cask was transferred, to equalise supplies between the boats, and a daily ration was set of three dippers-full per man, for it was clear that the stock of biscuits, corned beef, tinned fruit, and condensed milk would outlast the water. It was during that night that the lifeboats lost contact, and despite a show of flashing torches, were unable to regain it. While Chief Officer Underhill in No. 3 boat set a course north-northeast for the Cape Verdes, Captain Bibby aimed further south for Freetown, and it is he who takes up the story at this point: "After nine days in the boat we were picked up by the *Benvrackie*, and we continued in her until 0830 on 13th May about twenty miles north of the equator, steering in the direction of Walfish Bay, making about eleven knots and zig-zagging, when she was struck by two torpedoes. The torpedoes struck the engine room and No. 5 hold, and she disappeared in three minutes. Only one boat got away, and I was six hours in the water, wearing my life jacket and hanging on to a piece of wood. There were plenty of sharks around but they kept clear of the wreckage. I was eventually picked up by the boat and found it packed. There were fifty-eight of us in it and no room for more, but it sailed very well, and we again made for Freetown. Half the crew in the boat were Chinese and they were a little troublesome, agitating for more water. They were not rebellious, but as they were accustomed to drinking a lot of water, the ration of half a dipper seemed to worry them. One committed suicide by jumping overboard three times. We pulled him back twice but the third time he got away.

"After thirteen days in the boat, sailing 500 miles, we were picked up by the hospital ship *Oxfordshire*, which was bound for Freetown. It was dark at the time and we were showing our flares, which were seen on the hospital ship about seven miles away. Although we were cramped in the small boat and lost the use of our lower legs, we were able to walk up the ladder." Meanwhile, *Lassell*'s No. 3 lifeboat had been sailing southwest by east, as close to the wind as possible, and making two or three knots. With the salvaged stores from No. 2 life-

In port at Halifax, Nova Scotia, sailors of the Royal Navy and Merchant Navy enjoyed the hospitality of the Knights of Columbus All-Services Centre, as well as dances and other local entertainment in wartime.

boat, Chief Officer Underhill's supplies could have lasted for a month. There were ample cigarettes, but a dearth of matches, so when cigarettes were issued after the morning and evening "meals", one match was used to light the first and the rest were lit by mutual ignition, one fag to another. On 6th May it was decided that, with the wind northeast to east-northeast, they were never going to reach the Cape Verde Islands, and that their best course lay east, towards the convoy routes from Freetown—a choice which Captain Bibby had already taken. On 7th May, the wind dropped, the mainsail was lowered and the oars were manned, but thirty minutes rowing was enough to convince the men that such small progress as was made was not worth the effort. Biscuits, by then, had fallen out of favour as being too thirst-provoking. An alternative seemed to present itself when a squid, holding a flying fish in its tentacles, climbed aboard. So repellent, however, was the creature's aspect, with eyes bulging from a mottled, reddish head, that it was hurriedly cast back in the sea.

A few men needed medical attention, provided by a steward, for lacerations and abrasions; one suffered from sunburn and another seemed to lose the will to live. On the evening of the 8th May, two men sought permission to hold a short prayer meeting, and this was generally supported. The 2nd Steward led the company in the Lord's Prayer and, after a few moments of silent meditation, a prayer was offered up for urgent rescue—not only for them but for their shipmates in No. 1 lifeboat, whom they had not seen for eight days.

That lonely, heartfelt prayer was answered when daylight broke next morning, as the British liner *Egba* came over the horizon to the west. The company climbed her ladder, all but one without assistance, their sturdy boat was hoisted aboard the after deck, and *Egba* resumed her course for Freetown, passing *Lassell*'s empty No. 1 lifeboat on her way.

When Captain Bibby at last returned to England, he was required to make his report to the Admiralty's casualty section. In concluding it, he recommended that lifeboats should contain fewer biscuits and more water, praised the new kapok life jackets with red lights and whistles, and commented unfavourably on Freetown's facilities. "It is a very primitive place with little accommodation and an absence of suitable clothing. I would not put a dog in the hotel where I stayed." In this the Captain was at one with most merchant seamen, who normally referred to the port as Hitler's secret weapon.

In due course, Peter Guy returned to his first ship, the *Balfe*, and remained with her, still as a cadet, still learning seamanship the hard way, while she sailed the oceans of the world. At last, returning to London from another voyage to South America, he discovered that he had enough sea-time to qualify for a 2nd Mate's ticket—provided he could pass the examinations. The trouble was that, as he said, "I had never held a sextant or done any navigation work whatsoever, so I had to start from scratch." That meant a course of study at Sir John Cass College in London, and Lamport & Holt only paid a man for time at sea. It meant the dole for Guy, and luckily a billet near the college with a kindly aunt.

"There were a number of others like me, having to learn and work hard to do so. One day, during a coffee break, a naval officer came in. He said he was from the Admiralty, looking for keen, dashing young men to serve as navigation officers on destroyers, corvettes and the like. A number of us were attracted by the idea, and he went on to explain that first we had to get out of the Merchant Navy (a reserved occupation) and the way to do that was to volunteer for submarines, and that once we were in the Royal Navy, he would ensure that we got into escort vessels. A few days later an RAF officer came in and told us that, when he was at John Cass studying for his ticket like us, a naval officer had arrived with just such an offer, but with the difference that first he had to volunteer to be an RAF navigator. He had done that, and ever since he had been sitting over Berlin being fired at by all and sundry, and nursing a dream of meeting a certain naval officer in a dark alley somewhere."

All such snares and delusions avoided, Guy obtained his certificate. He returned to Lamport & Holt as 2nd Mate of the *Samarovsk*, and plied between Antwerp and Tilbury with war stores for the Allied armies until the war was won. Then it was marriage to his Wren sweetheart, and a decision that the time had come for him to swallow the anchor. It was a measure of how far he had travelled in the last six years that when he made one more voyage aboard his first ship, he found himself thinking of her as "the dear old *Balfe*."

A brief time out of war for Merchant Navy crewmen on convoy duty.

PICTURE CREDITS: PHOTOGRAPHS FROM THE AUTHOR'S COLLECTION ARE CREDITED—AC; THOSE FROM THE IMPERIAL WAR MUSEUM ARE CREDITED—IWM; FROM THE BUNDESARCHIV—BUNDES. P3-AC, P5-AC, P6-AC, P7-IWM, P8-AC, P9-IWM, P10-AC, P11-IWM, PP12-13-AC, P14 ALL-AC, P15-BUNDES, P17-AC, P19 TOP LEFT-AC, TOP RIGHT-BUNDES, BOTTOM-AC, P21-AC, P22-J. ARMSTRONG, P23-J. ARMSTRONG, P24 LEFT TO RIGHT-R. SEAGER, J. BELCHER, R. ATKINSON, P25 LEFT TO RIGHT-P. GUY, P. WAKKER, K. POLLARD, P26 ALL-AC, P27 BOTH-IWM, P28-AC, P29-IWM, P30-AC, P31-IWM, P32-PUBLIC ARCHIVES OF NOVA SCOTIA, P34-IWM, P35-AC, P37 ALL-AC, PP38-39 ALL-BUNDES, P45 ALL (EXCEPT CAP) BUNDES, CAP-AC, P47-AC, P48-BUNDES, P49-AC, P50-AC, P51 BOTH-AC, PP52-53-BUNDES, P54-AC, P55-AC, P56-BUNDES, P57-BUNDES, P59-NATIONAL ARCHIVES OF CANADA, P60-BUNDES, P61-AC, P62 ALL-AC, PP63-64 ALL-AC, P66-AC, P67-AC, PP68-69-AC, P70-IWM, P72-AC, PP74-75-AC, P76-AC, P79 BOTH-AC, P81-AC, P83 ALL-AC, P85-BUNDES, P86-BUNDES, P87-AC, P88-BUNDES, P90 BOTH-AC, P91-IWM, P92 ALL-AC, P93 BOTH-AC, P94-AC, P95 BOTH-AC, P96-NATIONAL ARCHIVES OF CANADA, P97 ALL-AC, P98 ALL-AC, P100-AC, P103-K. POLLARD, PP104-105-AC, P106-AC, P108-AC, P110-BUNDES, P111-BUNDES, P112-BUNDES, P115-P. GUY, P116-AC, P117 BOTH-AC, P118-NATIONAL ARCHIVES OF CANADA, P121-AC, P122-AC, P124 BOTH-PUBLIC ARCHIVES OF NOVA SCOTIA, P125- PUBLIC ARCHIVES OF NOVA SCOTIA, P127-IWM, P128-IWM.